WATERSIDE
In Stafforc

Roger Noyce

COUNTRYSIDE BOOKS
NEWBURY BERKSHIRE

First published 1999
© Roger Noyce 1999

COUNTRYSIDE BOOKS
3 Catherine Road
Newbury, Berkshire

ISBN 1 85306 555 2

Designed by Graham Whiteman
Cover illustration by Colin Doggett
Maps by the author
Photographs by Roger and Margaret Noyce

Produced through MRM Associates Ltd., Reading
Printed by J.W. Arrowsmith Ltd., Bristol

Contents

Introduction

Walk

1   Longnor and the Manifold Valley *(2½ miles)*   8

2   Meerbrook and Tittesworth Reservoir *(3¾ miles)*   13

3   Rudyard Reservoir Walk *(5 miles)*   17

4   Grindon and the Manifold Way *(3½ miles)*   21

5   Cheddleton and the Caldon Canal *(2½ miles)*   26

6   Etruria and the Two Canals Walk *(3½ miles)*   30

7   Consall Forge to Froghall Wharf *(5½ miles)*   34

8   The Trent & Mersey Canal and Barlaston *(3 miles)*   38

9   The Brooks of Milwich *(3½ miles)*   43

10   The River Dove at Tutbury *(2 miles)*   47

11   High Offley and the Shropshire Union Canal *(4 miles)*   50

12   The Trent Washlands and Burton upon Trent *(3 miles)*   54

13   Stafford's Heritage and the River Sow *(1½ miles)*   59

14   Great Haywood and the Meeting of Canals *(4 miles)*   64

AREA MAP SHOWING LOCATION OF THE WALKS

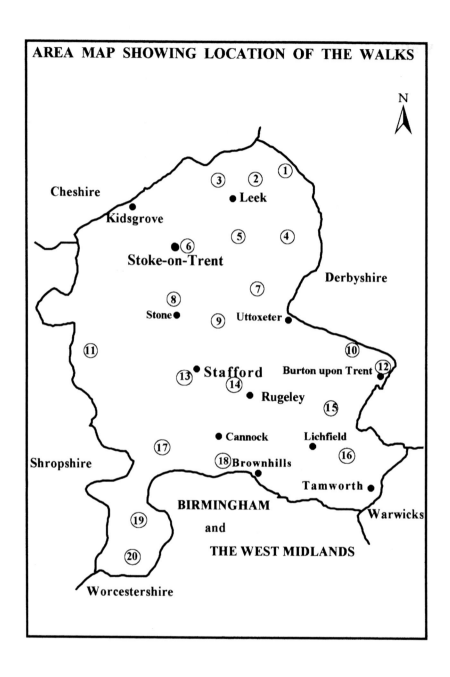

Walk

15 Picturesque Alrewas and its Waterways
(3 miles)   69

16 Whittington and the Coventry Canal *(3 miles)*   73

17 The Shropshire Union Canal and Brewood
(3 miles)   77

18 Chasewater and its Country Park *(3 miles)*   82

19 The Bratch Locks Walk and Trysull *(3½ miles)*   86

20 Kinver and the Staffordshire & Worcestershire
Canal *(4 miles)*   91

PUBLISHER'S NOTE
We hope that you obtain considerable enjoyment from this book; great care has been taken in its preparation. Although at the time of publication all routes followed public rights of way or permitted paths, diversion orders can be made and permissions withdrawn.

We cannot of course be held responsible for such diversion orders and any inaccuracies in the text which result from these or any other changes to the routes nor any damage which might result from walkers trespassing on private property. We are anxious though that all details covering the walks are kept up to date and would therefore welcome information from readers which would be relevant to future editions.

INTRODUCTION

The sparkle of a country river meandering through a scenic valley, the roar and attraction of a powerful waterfall, the delight of a colourful narrowboat passing under an ornate canal bridge, the peaceful reflections on beautiful lakes and reservoirs on a summer's day. These are a few of my favourite things which can be enjoyed in abundance in the fine county of Staffordshire.

Staffordshire is rightly proud of the fact that it has more rural canals than any other county in the UK and all of these canals now offer a variety of leisure interest for the walker. The Industrial Revolution saw the arrival of a number of major canals built to transport the many products of the industrial midlands and as a freight link for industry in the 18th century. These form a magnificent network covering much of Staffordshire. James Brindley was the main engineer building the Staffordshire & Worcestershire Canal in 1772 to transport coal, ironware, glass, pottery and textiles, also the Trent & Mersey Canal (finished in 1777) for transporting the china clay of Josiah Wedgwood and the Coventry Canal (finished in 1790) for carrying coal. Brindley also started the Caldon Canal which was completed by his brother-in-law Hugh Henshall in 1778. The Shropshire Union Canal was built by Thomas Telford to transport freight from the West Country to Ellesmere Port and the Birmingham & Fazeley Canal, engineered by John Smeaton, was completed in 1790 to form a link between Birmingham and the South-East. Up until the early 1900s these canals were busy commercial operations but with the advent of the motor car they fell into disuse and have now become a major leisure attraction offering a fascinating glimpse into history and easy walking access to the many picturesque villages in the county.

Three attractive rivers span Staffordshire. The River Trent flows from Burton upon Trent in the east, following the Trent & Mersey Canal to Stoke-on-Trent. The Manifold River meanders through Ilam on its path north up a beautiful valley on the east of Staffordshire while the delightful River Churnet carves its way from Rocester to Leek in the north. In addition, Blithfield, Chasewater, Rudyard and Tittesworth lakes/reservoirs provide fine scenery and a haven for wildlife.

The 20 walks in this book explore this feast of waterways. Part of each circuit endeavours to take the walker by the waterside to enjoy the scenic beauty and the routes also visit some of the most attractive villages in the county. The walks vary in length from $1\frac{1}{2}$ miles to just over $5\frac{1}{2}$ miles and should be within the walking capacity of the average person. The walking surface is generally very good so that persons of mature years and families with young children should have no difficulty. In dry weather the paths will be firm underfoot and normal outdoor footwear should be adequate. In wet weather, or during the winter months, there could be some moist stretches of footpaths when it is preferable to wear stout, waterproof boots or shoes.

There can be few greater pleasures of life than to combine a visit to a pub with a pleasant country stroll and to facilitate this each walk either starts from an attractive pub or passes a named pub en route. Details of parking facilities are provided together with information on the pub food and drinks available – the pub telephone number is included to enable you to make enquiries before your visit. Remember that you should always obtain the permission of the landlord if you intend to leave your vehicle in the pub car park. If you opt to park elsewhere, by the roadside perhaps, please make sure that you do not block any exits or entrances.

Brief details about places of interest within easy driving distance of each starting point are also given, to help you plan a full day out if you wish.

With each walk there is a sketch map which is intended to identify the starting point and should be adequate to guide you around the route. Ordnance Survey maps to the scale of 1:25 000 are specially designed for walkers and provide more detailed information. I recommend you to acquire the relevant Pathfinder, Explorer or Outdoor Leisure maps when walking these routes – details of these are included with each walk.

All of the routes incorporate public rights of way where there is an onus upon every walker to always follow the Country Code, to look after our precious countryside and to protect the environment for future generations.

I wish you happy waterside walking in the beautiful county of Staffordshire.

Roger Noyce

LONGNOR AND THE MANIFOLD VALLEY

This short walk starts from the delightful Peak District village of Longnor and offers superb views over the Manifold and Dove Valleys before descending for a stroll by the side of the fast running Manifold River.

The pub at the start of the walk.

Before you start the walk, why not spare time to stroll the narrow streets of Longnor – they all appear to end near the impressive old market hall which was built in 1873 and is now Longnor Craft Centre. Today the building is used to display products of local people and artists who work in and around the Peak District. The village church is a veritable treasure of fascinating ancient gravestones. Pause to read the headstone of William Billinge who died at the age of 112 in 1791 or recite one of the many quaint gravestone verses. My favourite is to the members of the Yates family buried between 1762 and 1789:

> *Stay mortals and depart not from this stone*
> *But stand and ponder whither we are gone*
> *Death quickly took our sense and strength away*
> *And laid us down upon this bed of clay*
> *Consider it! and take home this line*
> *The Grave that is made next, may be thine.*

The walk starts from the Crewe and Harpur Arms. It is ideally situated opposite Longnor Craft Centre in the centre of Longnor and has a good reputation for food and comfort – people travel regularly from Sheffield to visit! The pub was built in the 18th century by the Sir Harpur Crewe Estate of Calke Abbey and was initially used as a centre for payment of estate rents. Today everyone receives a warm welcome – and walkers in particular – in this Staffordshire part of the Peak District. The bar is open from 12 noon to 3 pm and from 6 pm to 11 pm during the week, all day at weekends. The real ales of Marston's Pedigree and Bitter are available, and the cider drinker can have Strongbow or Woodpecker from the cask.

Food is served from 12 noon to 3 pm and from 6 pm to 9 pm. The range varies from steaks, fish, pasta meals, omelettes and Indian or Chinese dishes to sandwiches and toasties. Each day there are specials available and on Sunday booking is required for the five-course lunch – a true favourite with visitors and locals alike.

There is a pleasant garden which has a patio area and there is a 'quiet pint' garden. Children are allowed in the pub and will enjoy the fine adventure playground. Dogs kept under control are welcome. The Crewe and Harpur Arms has overnight accommodation available on a B & B basis and there are also holiday cottages for rent.

Telephone: 01298 83205.

- **HOW TO GET THERE:** Longnor is situated to the north-east of Leek on the border with Derbyshire. Leave Leek on the A523 Ashbourne road, going left onto the B5053 road towards Buxton. The Crewe and Harpur Arms is on the street corner on the right as you enter Longnor.

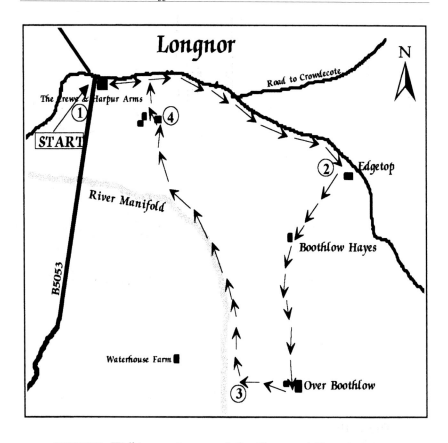

- **PARKING:** Walking customers of the Crew and Harpur Arms may leave their cars in the pub car park. Alternatively, there are parking places at the front of the Longnor Craft Centre, opposite the pub.
- **LENGTH OF THE WALK:** 2½ miles. Map: OS Outdoor Leisure 24 – The Peak District (White Peak Area) (GR 089649).

THE WALK

1. From the front of the Crewe and Harpur Arms, go right and walk along the pavement of the road for some 500 yards, then go right again down a quiet lane. There are pleasing views to the left of the Dove Valley and views to the right of the Manifold Valley. After walking along the lane for a further 500 yards pause to enjoy a particularly fine Dove Valley view to the left which embraces the small hamlet of Crowdecote.

The inconsequential stiles near Over Boothlow.

2. Go right over a stile in front of buildings at Edgetop. Walk the path going south/south-west, descending to go over a series of stiles with the path gently arcing left past Boothlow Hayes and with the Manifold Valley view now ahead of you.

   The path continues to arc left over fields and stiles, passing an old barn before arriving at a farm complex at Over Boothlow. Now, go right and descend a farm track going west towards the Manifold river.

3. At a pair of inconsequential stiles, go right and walk a path line now going north over a series of fields. The path proceeds over several stiles/gates and continues close to the river. After about a mile of riverside walking bear right over a stile then aim north/north-west towards a further stile set to the right of the farm complex at Folds End.

4. Go left through the farm gate and walk between the farm buildings then ascend the farm lane to reach the road on the edge of Longnor. Go left and in about 250 yards you will arrive back at the Crewe and Harpur Arms.

Places of Interest Nearby

Longnor Craft Centre in the old market hall (built 1873) contains a selection of craft. Telephone: 01298 83587. *Longnor Manifold Valley Patchwork*, Unit 2, Burton Road (by the fire station). Patchwork, embroidery and quilting displays. Telephone: 01298 83801. In *Buxton* (6½ miles north) places worth a visit include: the Opera House, Poole's Cavern, The Crescent and the Pavilion Gardens. Tourist Office: 01298 25106.

MEERBROOK AND TITTESWORTH RESERVOIR

✥

Pleasing Staffordshire countryside, superb hill views and a scenic reservoir form the basis of this fine short walk in the north of the county. The finale is a visit to the popular Tittesworth Reservoir which takes in the River Churnet and other small streams to supply Leek and Stoke-on-Trent with drinking water.

Tittesworth Reservoir.

Tittesworth Reservoir has been developed by Severn Trent to become a major visitor attraction in the area and locally it is known as the 'Loch of the Staffordshire Moorlands'. A beautiful reservoir to meander around, with attractive circular walks, it provides the opportunity to visit bird hides, a sensory garden and a chance to watch trout fishermen in action.

The walk starts from the Lazy Trout in Meerbrook, a historic pub which was built in 1650. Originally called the Three Horseshoes when it catered for the old cattle drovers, it has moved into the present day under a new name and has become a popular family-run village local that gives a warm welcome to walkers. Beer drinkers can enjoy a selection of real ales – among them Banks's and Marston's Pedigree – while a good range of ciders including Scrumpy Jack will appeal to the cider drinker. The bar is open all day on Saturdays from 11 am to 11 pm and on Sundays from noon to 10.30 pm. During the week drinking hours are from 11 am to 2.30 pm and 6 pm until 11 pm.

A full menu of food is always available including mixed grill, steaks, home-made lasagne and chilli. Every day, lunch is served from 11 am to 2.30 pm and evening meals are served from 6 pm to 8.30 pm, weekends from 6 pm to 9 pm. On Sundays roast dinners are served and these prove very popular although booking is not essential.

A Frenchman would feel at home drinking or eating at the tables at the front of the attractive Lazy Trout, while the picnic area at the rear always seems to have guests in the summer months. Children are allowed in the pub as are dogs but the latter must be on leads.

Telephone: 01538 300385.

- **HOW TO GET THERE:** Meerbrook is situated 3 miles north of Leek, off the A53 Leek to Buxton road. Follow the signposts westwards from the A53 to Meerbrook. The Lazy Trout is delightfully positioned in the middle of the village.
- **PARKING:** The Lazy Trout car park may be used by walkers by prior arrangement. Alternatively, you may park with consideration in the village of Meerbrook or in the pay & display car park at nearby Tittesworth Reservoir
- **LENGTH OF THE WALK:** 3¾ miles. Map: OS Outdoor Leisure 24 – The Peak District (White Peak Area) (GR 990608).

THE WALK

1. From the Lazy Trout, proceed ahead, walking past the YHA building to reach the front gate of the parish church. Enter the churchyard and go through a kissing gate at the rear of the church onto a narrow lane. Walk along this lane as it arcs right to reach a road. Here, go right and in 10 yards go left through a gate onto pastureland to join the Moorlands Walk. This is one of a series of 12 such circular walks on the Staffordshire

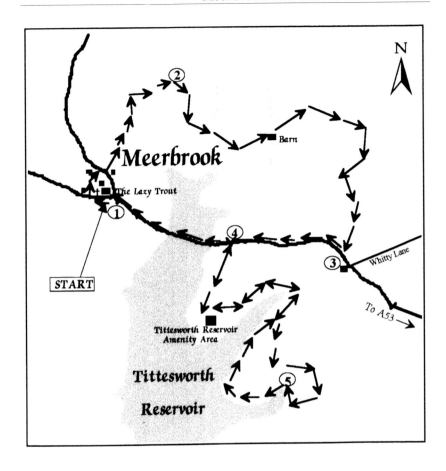

Moors, each covering a distance of between 3 and 12 miles and for which walk guides are available at local Tourist Offices. As you proceed in a generally north direction pause from time to time to enjoy retrospective glimpses of Tittesworth Reservoir. After the path veers right it becomes a stone track and ahead of you there is a truly magnificent view of The Roaches with the hump of Hen Cloud to its right. Walk along the track over a small stream and then go right below the buildings of Frith Bottom.

2. Continue following the Moorlands Walk waymarkers initially going south-east and then turning left over a stile towards The Roaches once again. After going over a stile by a small stone

15

barn you will veer right and can then follow a series of tall red marker posts which will guide you over several stiles and fields going south. After going over further stiles you will reach the road in Middle Hulme.

3. Go right and walk the quiet road for about 600 yards to reach the entrance gates to Severn Trent's Tittesworth Reservoir (open from 7.30 am to 9.30 pm).

4. Go left and enter the reservoir area to reach the impressive Visitor Centre. The reservoir is a superb trout lake which offers a number of attractive trails. The Short Trail commences a delightful part of this walk. Follow the very clear 'Short Trail' markers which will take you around the north-east section of the reservoir, then you descend by the water to enter woodland and go over a couple of footbridges over streams. At the most southerly point you could choose to walk the Long Trail – this goes all of the way around the lake to exit onto the road near to Meerbrook and you should allow a further 2½ hours if you decide upon this longer walk.

5. When returning on the Short Trail bear left at a crossroads of paths on leaving the woodland and walk along the reservoir bank up the east side of the lake to arrive back at the Visitor Centre.

   From the reservoir go left along the road and ascend into the village of Meerbrook to return to the Lazy Trout.

Places of Interest Nearby

Brindley Mill is about 4 miles away and situated just north of Leek on the A523 (Leek to Macclesfield) road. It is a working water-powered corn mill built by James Brindley in 1752 by the side of the River Churnet. Displays illustrate the life and work of the famous engineer and the history of milling. Leek Tourist Office: 01538 483741.

RUDYARD RESERVOIR WALK

The beautiful Rudyard Lake was built in 1796 as a canal feeder reservoir designed to supply the Caldon Canal. Although not a natural lake it has become an important site for wildlife and a leisure lake for everyone to enjoy. This easy walk embraces stretches of the Staffordshire Way and the Moorlands Walk as it circles the lake offering fine views with yachts and other small craft adding colour to the beauty of the scene. A special day out.

Rudyard Lake.

The pretty village of Rudyard, set at the south end of lovely woods bordering the lake, is well known for its connection with Rudyard Kipling, the famous novelist and poet. In the 1860s, a certain Lockwood Kipling and Alice MacDonald regularly visited the village to walk in the woods and along the banks of the beautiful lake. They became engaged to be married when in Rudyard and their son was named after the village. Today, walking past well tended gardens and strolling the shore of Rudyard Reservoir continues to be a delight.

The walk starts from the Poachers Tavern in Rudyard. Walkers are assured of a warm welcome in this privately owned freehouse which in part dates from 1610. One guest ale and Strongbow cider are on tap daily from 12 noon to 3 pm and from 7 pm to 11 pm and it is a delight to imbibe on the patio or in the garden from either of which there is a pleasing view over the local countryside.

If good food is your desire you will enjoy the quality fresh produce which goes into the à la carte and lunchtime bar meals. The lunch menu has a selection of superb bar snacks which are available from 12 noon to 2 pm each day in the restaurant, the bar area, the garden or on the patio. Evening meals are served between 7 pm and 9.30 pm. The inn is very popular and booking is required for Sunday lunch. Children may join you in the pavilion restaurant area at lunchtime. Dogs (on leads) are only allowed in the outside areas.

Telephone: 01538 306294.

- **HOW TO GET THERE:** Rudyard is situated north-west of Leek off the A523 road towards Macclesfield. About 2 miles along the A523, turn left onto the B5331 road signed 'Rudyard'. The Poachers Tavern is on the left at the main road junction in the village.
- **PARKING:** The Poachers Tavern car park may be used by walking customers with prior agreement. Alternatively there is a public car park by the bridge on the entry to Rudyard.
- **LENGTH OF THE WALK:** 5 miles. Map: OS Outdoor Leisure 24 – The Peak District (White Peak Area). (GR 954577).

THE WALK

1. From the Poachers Tavern, descend the B5331 road. Go left through a metal kissing gate sited to the left of a petrol station. Walk along the footpath by the side of a stream with pastureland and often highland cattle to the right. In about 500 yards ascend to the south end of Rudyard Reservoir where you will enjoy a fine view of the lake. Go right and proceed over the dam bridge, then go left to join the Moorlands Walk route (see Walk 2) and to walk 2 miles along a dismantled railway track which runs along the east side of this beautiful reservoir. This track was once the LM&S Macclesfield to Uttoxeter line and today contains the narrow gauge rail line

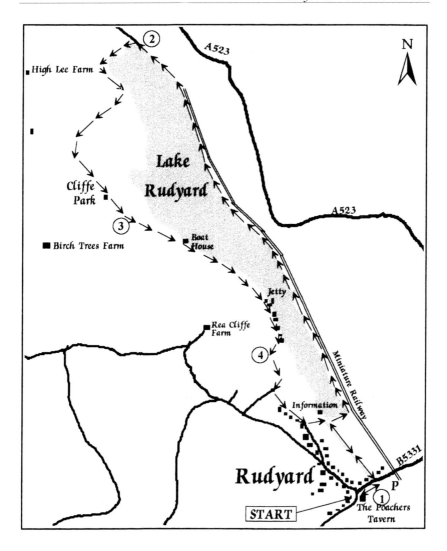

for a miniature steam railway running between the old Rudyard Lake Station (by the alternative car park) and the north end of the lake. This is an easy stretch of walking with pleasing views of the lake - the jetty on the opposite bank is a very attractive feature.

2. At the end of the wide track go left under a bridge for a fine view from the end of the reservoir. You are now on the

19

Staffordshire Way, and will pass by a small car park to walk along the farm drive towards High Lee Farm. You pass some sheds/huts on the right and go over a stile on the driveway to farm buildings now visible to the right ahead. As the drive ascends by trees, go left on a double tarmac strip drive heading towards Cliffe Park – an impressive private house built in 1811. Walk along the tarmac drive through the house grounds and continue along a track lined with lime trees to enjoy good views over the lake.

3. Proceed over a stile into Rea Cliffe Wood and continue in a south-east direction to reach Cliffe Park Lodge – the old fortified lodge gates to the big house which are now sadly in poor repair. On the lake bank is the Rudyard Lake Sailing Club premises. Continue past the jetty and past some lakeside houses and soon the track bends sharp right.

4. In about 70 yards, go left, continuing to follow the Staffordshire Way waymarkers, on a path through the trees. The path gradually arcs right to a lane by houses and when you have passed The Villa continue along a hedged path to the right of a caravan site into Rea Cliffe Wood again, eventually passing to the rear of a row of terraced houses. Soon you will enter Lake Road where you go left through a gate to descend a path to the information centre by Rudyard Lake dam.

   Go right and descend to walk by the stream as you return to the Poachers Tavern via the path on which you started the walk.

Places of Interest Nearby
Biddulph Grange Garden and Country Park (4½ miles away with access from the A527 north of Biddulph). National Trust themed gardens which give you a taste of China, America, Egypt and Italy. Telephone: 01782 517999. *Little Moreton Hall* (7½ miles away, south of Congleton on the A34). A magnificent National Trust 15th-century Tudor manor house, with superb patterned black and white timbering, a dazzling structure and architectural curiosity. Telephone: 01260 272018.

GRINDON AND THE MANIFOLD WAY

Sitting high on the Staffordshire Moorlands, Grindon (recorded in the Domesday Book as Grendon – meaning 'green hill') provides fine views embracing the White Peak area. This circular route descends through attractive valleys to walk along the Manifold Way within sight of Thor's Cave, then ascends most beautiful hills to return to the village.

The village pub at Grindon.

The unspoilt and somewhat isolated village of Grindon offers the peace of a bygone age and it is a pleasure to meander along its quiet lanes. All Saints is a Gothic church which tends to be the central feature and is sometimes referred to as the 'Cathedral of the Moors'. It was built in 1848 on a site of several earlier churches. Originally, the Chapel of Ilam was built in the 11th century only to be replaced in the 16th/17th century by a small square-towered church with free school attached. Today the church retains a series of interesting gargoyles positioned on the west and south corners of the building.

The walk starts from the 16th-century Cavalier Inn – it was originally a local smithy but has survived to become the only public house in this rural village. Ramblers are very welcome in this walking area of the county and the inn caters for the summer visitor by keeping open seven days a week during the main walking period of the year – it can get very busy. In winter the inn is likely to be open only at weekends. The real ales on tap are normally Wards and Bass together with a range of guest beers. Strongbow cider is also on draught as are Labatt's and Carling Black lagers.

The bar snack menu may be taken in either the bar or the dining room and there is a wide selection of sandwiches and fillings which are likely to suit the walker. Gammon, sirloin and rump steaks and speciality home-made burgers tend to be favourite in the dining room while fish invariably appears on the menu. The landlord is happy to cater for walking groups but does ask for advance bookings to be made. The pub is open for food and drinks from 12 noon to 3 pm and from 7 pm to 11 pm.

Children are welcome and can entertain themselves in the play area in the beer garden. Dogs are not allowed on the premises.

Telephone: 01538 304285.

- **HOW TO GET THERE:** Grindon is a remote village set to the east of Leek. It is best approached on the A523 Leek to Ashbourne road. At the village of Winkhill take the road going north-east signed 'Grindon'. Follow the signposting into the village and you will find the Cavalier Inn on the right.
- **PARKING:** Walking customers of the Cavalier Inn may park in the pub car park with prior agreement. There is also a free car park by the side of St Edward's church.
- **LENGTH OF THE WALK:** Just over 3½ miles. Map: OS Outdoor Leisure 24 – The Peak District (White Peak Area) (GR 085543).

THE WALK

1. From the Cavalier Inn, cross the road to walk along the lane opposite. Pass by Rose Cottage (on the right) and then go left, descending a lane towards a row of terraced houses. Before the first house on the right, go right over a stile onto a path

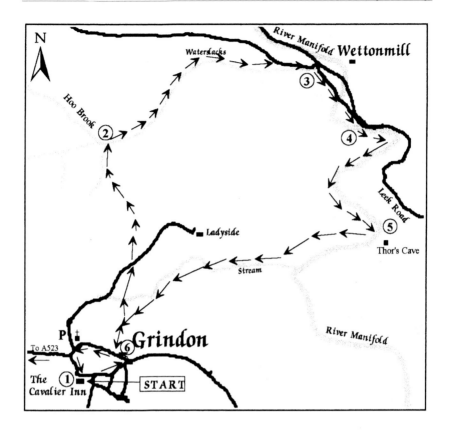

going generally north. The path descends over a midfield footpath then ascends over a hedge stile. Aim for the next field corner to go over a stile onto a farm drive, which you cross, and proceed over the stile opposite onto a bridlepath. Walk the bridlepath as it descends over stiles/gates into the valley below and enjoy the pleasing view ahead. Shortly after you hear Hoo Brook babbling on your left, go right over a footbridge over the brook and follow the bridleway waymark to Wettonmill.

2. Continue now in a north-east direction on a clear path through attractive valley pastureland with Hoo Brook close by on your right for the next ¾ mile. You will go through a mid-valley gate and past waterslacks set in the brook to prevent branches and other debris drifting downstream. This is a delightful and

easy stretch of valley walking with wild flowers adding further colour as you approach the Manifold Valley.

3. At the valley end cross over a lane (the Wetton road) to visit Wettonmill, where refreshments can be enjoyed or you may choose to ascend to one of the rock caves. Return to cross over the Wetton road and now bear left to cross the ford over the adjacent lane. This quiet lane runs parallel to the Wetton road but without traffic. (If the ford is impassable you will need to walk along the narrow Wetton road where there are car-passing places.) This is a very pleasant, easy walk by the side of the River Manifold with rocky crags to your left.

4. Where the lane meets the Wetton road, go right over a bridge over the River Manifold to walk the Manifold Way – a tarmac track which winds its way south by the River Manifold. In winter the water will flow rapidly but in the summer the river can dry up. For a length of its route to Ilam it is an underground river which overflows in wet/winter weather to form the Manifold River we expect to see.

    After walking the Way for about ¾ mile you will see a footbridge to the left and Thor's Cave is clearly visible in the rocky crag above. Named after Thor, the Norse God of Thunder, the view from the 40 ft wide mouth of the cave provides a superb panorama of the surrounding countryside. In the 19th century Samuel Carrington, a local school teacher, discovered flint arrow heads, bone combs, bronze bracelets and brooches and a Roman coin in the cave. Today, the inside of the cave is a dank chamber and rather uninviting – it is not hard to believe that human remains were once discovered here. The entrance is an interesting feature which is rather like a Norman arched doorway. Walk onto the footbridge to enjoy the view and/or to ascend to visit the cave.

5. Leave the footbridge and return to the Manifold Way, crossing over the tarmac track and going over a stile opposite to enter a National Trust area called Ladyside. Proceed in a south-west direction until you return to the village of Grindon. Initially there is a short, steep ascent through the trees of Ladyside Wood and then a more gentle ascent of an open area, walking

to the right of a fence. Then you go left over a stile to walk a balcony type path through the woods to enjoy periodic fine views over the Manifold Valley to your left. Exit the woods via a stile, then go left over a wall-stile to walk to the right of trees over undulating pastureland, initially keeping the brook on your left. Soon you will see the spire of All Saints' church in Grindon and will go over a stile to ascend pastureland and join the same path on which you started your walk.

6. At the lane in the village, go right to arrive at the church and to see the Rindle Stone, a stone pillar set near to the church gates – it bears the following inscription, 'The Lord of the Manor of Grindon established his right to this Rindle at Stafford Assizes on March 17th 1862'. (A rindle is a brook flowing only in wet weather.) Spend a few minutes to see the fascinating gargoyles on the corners of the church building then descend the lane back to the Cavalier Inn.

Places of Interest Nearby

Blackbrook at Winkhill, situated just off the A523 between Leek and Ashbourne, is an interesting zoological park. Telephone: 01538 308293. *Ilam Park* (about 5 miles south of Grindon) is a 50 acre National Trust property which is open all year to visitors. Telephone: 01335 350245. *Dovedale* (east of Grindon) is a delightful part of the Peak District where the beautiful River Dove flows through a superb valley between attractive rock formations and woodland.

CHEDDLETON AND THE CALDON CANAL

Cheddleton is a pleasant town, probably best known for its historic flint mill which is situated adjacent to the delightful Caldon Canal. This easy walk starts near Cheddleton Railway Centre, then takes you into the old town before descending for a visit to the flint mill and concludes with a delightful towpath walk between the Caldon Canal and the River Churnet.

The canalside inn at Cheddleton.

The A520 divides the town of Cheddleton to the south of the River Churnet and the Caldon Canal. St Edward's 12th-century parish church is the main feature of the old village and sits high above the Churnet Valley to provide a good view of the canal. The restored flint mill is a real treasure where one can watch two waterwheels driving the old flint grinding machinery. In the late 18th century the two unique undershot wheels were used to grind flint powder for use in the ceramics industry and then the powder was transported by canal barge to the Potteries. Today it is a Grade II listed building containing a collection of exhibits relating to the pottery industry which take one back to a bygone era. Telephone 01782 502907 for details of opening times.

The Gothic style Cheddleton Railway Station building was opened in 1849 during the Industrial Revolution and is attributed to Augustus Pugin, one of the architects of the House of Commons. By the 1950s and 1960s the line saw extensive use in freight and excursion traffic but sadly was later closed by the Beeching axe. The handsome Victorian railway station became a Grade II listed building in the 1970s and involved in this was Sir John Betjeman, the poet laureate. There has been a recent revival of the steam engine through the Churnet Valley Railway Society and in 1998 the railway began running again from Leekbrook through Cheddleton to Consall. The station complete with original booking hall and ticket office provides a nostalgic scene. Telephone 01538 360522 for times of opening.

Nearby, the Boat Inn is a delightful canalside pub where walkers are particularly welcomed. Built around 1700 and adorned with colourful flowers in summer months, it is an attractive place, and on warm days a drink and/or bar snack at the outside picnic tables is a very pleasant experience. Throughout the summer drinks are available from 12 noon to 3 pm and from 6 pm to 11 pm. Marston's Pedigree and Bitter are the real ales from the cask and Strongbow is the dry cider on tap.

A full bar menu is available and there is a specials board. Steaks and vegetarian meals are popular but steak with Stilton cheese is a local favourite. Food is served from 12 noon to 1.45 pm and from 6 pm to 8.30 pm during the summer – booking is not required for Sunday lunch. Cheddleton is a very rural place and the opening hours may be shorter during winter months. Children may eat inside the inn and at the picnic tables outside. Dogs are only allowed if they are kept under control. Telephone: 01538 360683.

- **HOW TO GET THERE:** Cheddleton is situated just to the south of Leek and is best approached from Leek on the A520 (Leek to Stone) road. Just before crossing over the River Churnet, go left and follow the signs to the North Staffordshire Railway Museum.

27

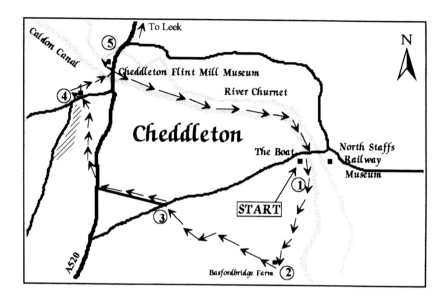

- **PARKING:** Customers of the Boat may park in the pub car park sited on the other side of the Caldon Canal – the car park will be locked outside the pub's opening hours. Alternatively, there is a public car park and picnic area sited between the North Staffs Railway Museum and the River Churnet.
- **LENGTH OF THE WALK:** 2½ miles. Map: OS Outdoor Leisure 24 – The Peak District (White Peak Area) (GR 981521).

THE WALK

1. Leave the Boat Inn over a stile at the back of the pub and walk along a path initially by the side of the Caldon Canal. The path ascends to go through a gate and pulls away from the canal – from the path there is a fine view over the canal and the River Churnet with the moorlands forming the backdrop. The path continues to the right of a hedge until it reaches the buildings of Basfordbridge Farm.

2. Go right up the farm track between the farm and its buildings to reach the brow of the hill on a lane by a wall. A wide panoramic view of the area unfolds as does the town of Cheddleton ahead. Continue along the lane as its bends right to reach a road opposite houses.

3. Cross over the road and walk up The Avenue opposite to the main road. Go right by the Londis supermarket then cross over the A520 to walk along a residential road named Ox Pasture. When the road bends left continue ahead along a hedged footpath at the back of the houses. Soon the path has more open surroundings and a fine view offers towards Combes Valley Nature Reserve. At the footpath end, cross a road to enter St Edward's churchyard.

4. Exit the churchyard via steps at the rear and go right to walk along a clear path to reach a residential lane. At the lane, go left immediately after a domestic car garage and descend a steep narrow fenced path down to the road by Cheddleton Flint Mill. Go left along the side of the Caldon Canal to reach the fantastic Flint Mill.

5. Leaving the Flint Mill, return to walk the canal towpath beneath bridge No 42, passing by a pair of superb lock gates and then continuing between the canal and the River Churnet. This is an easy and delightful stretch of walking to return to bridge No 44 and the Boat Inn.

ETRURIA AND THE TWO CANALS WALK

࿔❦࿔

A delightful walk along the towpath of two of James Brindley's famous canals with an opportunity to appreciate the fine engineering. A stroll through Hanley Park offers a lakeside venture into an area of colourful flowers. This is an attractive short countryside walk set in the Potteries city of Stoke-on-Trent.

The pub garden overlooking the marina.

Synonymous with Stoke-on-Trent are the famous pottery making names of Wedgwood, Minton, Copeland, Spode and Coalport who still dominate north Staffordshire after some 100/150 years. Originally they dominated the six towns of Tunstall, Burslem, Hanley, Longton, Fenton and Stoke which in 1910 joined together to become the city of Stoke-on-Trent. Josiah Wedgwood, 'the Father of the Pottery Industry', had already built an entire village for his employees and had called it Etruria. At the beginning of the Second World War, subsidence affected the Etruria site and the Wedgwood factory moved to Barlaston following which the Etruria area became somewhat desolate. Happily an award-winning land reclamation scheme revived Etruria and it became the venue for the famous National Garden Festival in 1986. Today the Festival Park is a popular visitor attraction with a wide variety of activities available.

The walk starts from the China Garden which is a feature of Festival Park. Visitors gain much pleasure from dining and drinking at the canalside tables overlooking the narrowboats which congregate in the marina. This popular Toby inn was built for the Garden Festival and provides easy access to the canal towpaths via a drawbridge which has to be raised to let boats in and out of the marina.

Bass and Worthington real ales are a big attraction for the beer drinker here while Dry Blackthorn and Sweet Woodpecker will quench the thirst of the cider drinker. Wine is available by the glass. In the summer months (May to September) the inn is open all day, every day. Food and drinks are also available all day at weekends throughout the winter. From October to April the weekday opening times are 11.30 am to 3 pm and 5.30 pm to 11 pm, with food available from 12 noon to 2 pm and 5.30 pm to 10 pm.

The Toby carvery, which includes all of the traditional fresh trimmings, is a favourite on the China Garden menu. Other menu items change twice a year – of these 8 oz sirloin steaks, salmon with dill sauce and breaded scampi are regular attractions and who could resist a lemon sponge pudding or rhubarb and apple crumble?

This is a friendly place and walkers are particularly welcome. Children are allowed in the inn but dogs must remain outside the building. The large garden area is a scenic and popular delight with customers.

Telephone: 01782 260199.

- **HOW TO GET THERE:** Stoke-on-Trent is to the north-east of junction 15 of the M6 motorway and is best approached from there on the A500 road. Follow the signs to the city centre and then for the Festival Park. At the park go left signposted 'Marina and Entertainment' – the China Garden will be on your left.
- **PARKING:** There is a large car park at the China Garden which is available to walking customers.

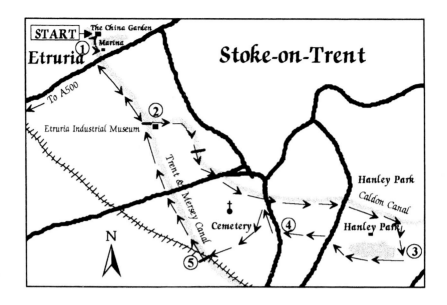

- **LENGTH OF THE WALK:** 3½ miles. Map: OS Pathfinder 809 – Stoke-on-Trent (GR 869474).

THE WALK

1. Leave the inn via the small drawbridge over the boat entrance for the marina and walk along the towpath of the Trent & Mersey Canal, bearing left to pass the marina and to reach the canal bridge. Ascend the steps to the left of the bridge, cross over the canal and descend the other side to proceed under the bridge and to continue on the towpath which is now on the right side of the canal. In about ¼ mile you will reach the junction of the Trent & Mersey and Caldon Canals at lock gates. Cross the bridge over the Trent & Mersey and go to the left of the buildings of the Etruria Industrial Museum to join the towpath of the Caldon Canal.

2. Walk on the towpath of the Caldon Canal for about ¾ mile. You will pass beneath a series of canal bridges as you proceed at the back of factories and houses – the canal is fairly narrow and a meeting of narrowboats is an interesting sight. After you have walked beneath bridge 5A, Hanley Park will be on each side of the canal. Go right through a gate to enter the park,

passing by a bowling green and tennis courts to reach a small lake.

3. Proceed to the left of the lake and walk along its far bank. At the lake end bear right to go through gates over a road into an attractive area of flowerbeds and borders.

4. Leave the park via a further large gate and go right, then left to enter the city cemetery. Walk the tarmac path through the cemetery, aiming generally towards its far left-hand corner. There you can exit the cemetery via a gate into Avenue Road. Go right along the pavement by iron railings to pass by a terraced row of private houses with private garages at their rear and to arrive at a footbridge over the railway.

5. Cross over the footbridge, bearing left to descend to the towpath of the Trent & Mersey Canal. Go left and walk past an iron milepost – Preston Brook 36 miles – beneath the bridge. In about 200 yards you will pass two bottle-shaped brick ovens on your left. These ovens were a common sight in the 19th century but are sadly all that remains of a sizeable pottery complex – opposite you will see the cemetery. Continue along the towpath, going beneath the very low road bridge by Twyford Lock to reach the lock gates by Etruria Industrial Museum.

Continue along the towpath, crossing over the canal to return to the China Garden.

Places of Interest Nearby
Pottery Factory Visitor Centres – no visit to Stoke-on-Trent would be complete without visiting one of the many famous local potteries: Royal Doulton, Nile St, Burslem (telephone: 01782 292434); Spode, Spode Works, Church St, Stoke (telephone: 01782 744011); Wedgwood, Barlaston (telephone: 01782 204218). *Gladstone Pottery Museum*, Uttoxeter Road, Longton. At this working museum you can see how 19th-century potters worked. The cobbled yard and huge bottle-shaped kilns are a quaint step back in history. Telephone: 01782 319232. *Etruria Industrial Museum*, Lower Bedford St, Etruria. Steaming weekends take place when 'Princess' an 1820 beam engine supplied with steam by a coal-fired 1903 boiler, drives an 1856 grinding machine. A resident blacksmith displays the skills of yesteryear in the Blacksmith's Forge. Telephone: 01782 287557.

CONSALL FORGE TO FROGHALL WHARF

This walk from Consall Forge starts with a tranquil towpath stroll before ascending through attractive woodland to the hamlet of Hazlescross and a wildlife sanctuary. The route then returns to the Caldon Canal towpath to continue to Froghall Wharf. The wharf is the very end of the canal and is a scenic pleasure to enjoy before returning along the towpath to Consall.

The Black Lion pub.

Consall Forge is a tiny hamlet which during the Industrial Revolution bustled with a variety of mineral works along the banks of the River Churnet. Today all that remains of the industrial background is a bank of overgrown lime kilns sited near to the car parking area. Consall Forge has become a quiet backwater - a peaceful, beautiful place which is only occasionally ruffled by the occasional passing narrowboat or by a steam train on the Churnet Valley Railway. It is here where the River Churnet and the Caldon Canal split over a fine weir that the inviting Black Lion pub provides the backcloth to a magical scene.

The walk starts from the Black Lion where walkers are particularly welcome and Marston's Pedigree, Speckled Hen and Titanic real ales are an attraction. Scrumpy Jack and Woodpecker ciders are on tap too while house and listed wines are also available. One can think of few greater pleasures on a warm day than imbibing at one of the picnic tables overlooking the beautiful waterside scene. At weekends the bar is open from 12 noon to 11 pm and during the week drinks are available from 12 noon to 3 pm and 6.30 pm to 11 pm.

The food menu includes steaks, chops, fish, chicken and vegetarian meals with Indian balti and curries a speciality. This is a popular pub with local people although no bookings are taken on Sundays when food is served from 12 noon to 4 pm and 6.30 pm to 9 pm. The same food hours operate on Saturdays but during the week the hours are 12 noon to 2.30 pm and 6.30 pm to 9 pm. Well-behaved children are always welcome in the Black Lion but no dogs are allowed.

Telephone: 01782 550294.

- **HOW TO GET THERE:** Consall is a small village situated to the south of Leek off the A520 (Leek to Stone) road. Go onto the A522 at Wetley Rocks and follow the signs to Consall on a minor road. Proceed through the village of Consall onto a lane going east. Follow the lane, passing by Consall Wood Visitor Centre onto a stone track which leads to the Black Lion pub on the bank of the Caldon Canal.
- **PARKING:** There is free car parking available to walkers on the bank of the River Churnet.
- **LENGTH OF THE WALK:** Just over 5½ miles. Map: OS Pathfinder 810 – Ashbourne and The Churnet Valley (GR 000491).

THE WALK

1. From the Black Lion, walk the towpath of the Caldon Canal, going past the Consall railway station. In about ¾ mile you will pass the Consall Forge Pottery to reach a bridge over the canal. Cross over the canal and the railway lane and ascend through Hazles Wood, following the red walk waymarkers of

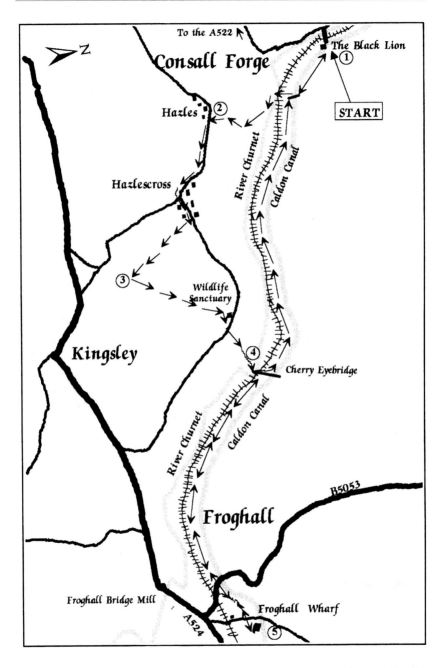

Froghall Wharf Walks. This is a short but steep ascent to arrive on Hollins Lane near to the hamlet of Hazles.

2. Go left along the lane to reach the neighbouring hamlet of Hazlescross. At the road junction go left into the hamlet then, in some 100 yards, go right through a gate into open countryside. Continue south-east over two fields and a stile into a third field.

3. Look out for a red waymarker in about 60 yards directing north-east and continue over fields to reach a gate into the woods set immediately to the right of the wildlife sanctuary. As you descend the hill steps, the sanctuary is close on the left and they have light refreshments available. Continue to descend the hill through woodland, then go across a footbridge over the River Churnet and the railway line to reach the Caldon Canal at bridge No 53.

4. Go right and walk the canal towpath into Froghall. You will pass a huge factory complex before arriving at bridge No 54 – the B5053 goes over the canal here. The attractive Froghall Wharf picnic site is reached after going around a short tunnel (76 yards long and with 6 foot headroom for the narrow-boats). The wharf marks the very end of the 17 mile long Caldon Canal.

5. After taking time to enjoy the wharf scene return along the towpath of the canal. This 2 mile walk starts on the left bank of the canal, crossing over to the right bank at bridge No 48. Bridge No 53 is Cherry Eyebridge which got its name from the condition of ironstone miners' eyes when emerging from their tunnels. You will pass by the remains of Consall Upper Flint Mills and the new railway station of Consall before arriving at the Black Lion at Consall Forge.

Places of Interest Nearby
Consall Nature Park offers nature displays, exhibitions and superb walking in the Churnet Valley. *Froghall Wharf* is a delightful scene at the end of the Caldon Canal. Canal boat trips are available (telephone: 01538 266486).

THE TRENT & MERSEY CANAL
AND BARLASTON

This easy short walk starts from the Duke of York pub in the pleasant village of Barlaston and embraces a delightful stroll along the towpath of the Trent & Mersey Canal. After leaving the canal one can pause and enjoy a scenic lake view before returning to the village.

Cottages on the bank of the Trent & Mersey Canal.

Until the start of the Second World War, Barlaston was a sleepy village. When the new Wedgwood factory at Barlaston commenced production in 1940 the picture changed as the railway and the Trent & Mersey Canal became important means of transportation for the famous pottery. The Wedgwood Group is the largest china and earthenware manufacturer in the world and the Barlaston factory is at the centre of the industry with its six 'clean' electric tunnel ovens.

The Duke of York is the village pub in Barlaston. About 200 years ago the building was a row of four cottages but the frontage of the cottages was altered and the buildings were converted to its present use. It is a pleasant inn which has beams and horse brasses in its very comfortable lounge and bar. Draught Bass and cask Worthington are the real ales which are on tap all day at weekends and from 11 am to 4.30 pm and 6 pm to 11 pm on weekdays. Strongbow cider is available in the bottle and wine can be bought by the glass or bottle.

The well-prepared food at the Duke of York is ideal refreshment before or after a pleasant walk in the countryside around Barlaston and along the canal towpath. A full bar snack menu is on offer at lunchtime from Monday to Saturday between the hours of 12 noon and 2.30 pm when home-made soup is a speciality of the house. On Sunday filled rolls are the only food available. If you are walking with a group could you please book in advance.

Children are allowed in the pub during the day and there are picnic benches in a yard to the side of the car park where you can enjoy a village scene – the post office is almost opposite. Dogs (under control) are only allowed in the bar area.

Telephone: 01782 374221.

- **HOW TO GET THERE:** Barlaston is to the north of Stone and set to the east of Tittensor off the A34 road. After crossing over the Trent & Mersey Canal and the main railway line enter the centre of Barlaston. Turn left just past the library and the Duke of York is on the right.
- **PARKING:** Walking customers may park in the pub car park at the Duke of York but do advise the landlord before you depart on the walk. Alternatively, park with care by the side of the road near the library in Barlaston.
- **LENGTH OF THE WALK:** 3 miles. Map: OS Pathfinder 830 – Stone (Staffs) (GR 894384).

THE WALK

1. From the Duke of York, go left and descend the pavement of Longton Road towards the large village green. Near the road junction, go right and walk in front of the village library (the former school built in 1680). About 150 yards beyond the library cross over the road and go left to enter a track set to the right of the modern parish church of St John the Baptist. Walk the clear track as it proceeds generally south-west to the

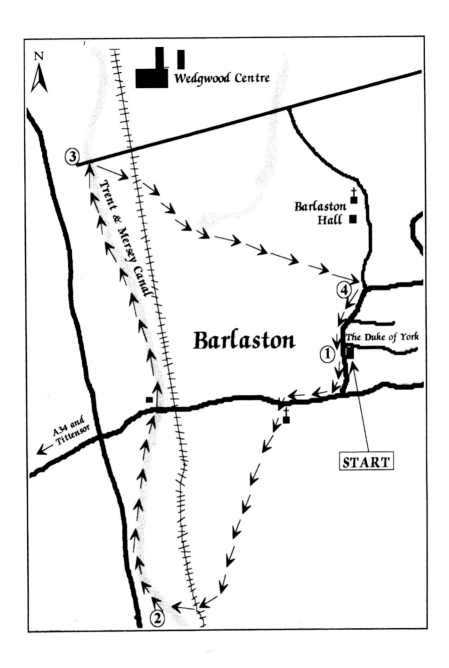

The village pub, Barlaston.

left of a hedge – it becomes a path over pastureland as it continues to the right of a field hedge. Look out for a stile on the left to go through the hedge onto a track which leads right below a railway bridge.

2. Cross over the bridge across the Trent & Mersey Canal and go left to descend to its towpath. Continue left beneath the bridge and commence a delightful $1\frac{1}{4}$ miles of attractive towpath walking. You will soon be at the rear of beautiful residential gardens which have pleasingly spread onto the towpath to provide floral enjoyment. After passing beneath the bridge by the Plume & Feather Inn the towpath continues north with the peaceful scene occasionally broken by an inter-city train speeding along the nearby railway line. As one approaches the canal bridge near the Wedgwood Centre one can so easily imagine Wedgwood barges drawn by horses and carrying the famous pottery to Birmingham.

3. Leave the canal at Oldroad Bridge (No 104), and go immediately right through a field corner gate to commence a pastureland walk back to the village of Barlaston. You will go through a pair of kissing gates to cross the rail line and then go over stiles to walk at the bottom end of a beautiful small lake near to Cresswell Wood. Ascend the field from the lake

and you will have a most superb view of Barlaston Hall to the left ahead. This fine mid-18th-century building was the headquarters of the Bank of England during the Second World War. In 1773 a picture of the Hall appeared on a dinner service made for the Empress Catherine of Russia. Today it is privately owned and closed to the public. The path leads over stiles to a kissing gate onto Longton Road by a junction with the lane to the Wedgwood Centre.

4. Go right and meander down Longton Road, walking past some very attractive houses on the right before reaching the Duke of York public house at the corner of Vicarage Lane.

Places of Interest Nearby
Wedgwood Visitor Centre is just off the walk route at Barlaston. Telephone: 01782 204218. *Trentham Gardens* (2½ miles north-west of Barlaston) – once the county seat for the Dukes of Sutherland – comprises some 800 acres of superb parkland. There are fine gardens and a lake. Telephone: 01782 657341.

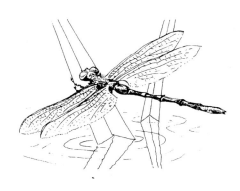

THE BROOKS OF MILWICH

The peaceful village of Milwich is surrounded by babbling brooks and pretty countryside and is a popular starting place for walking groups. This pleasant walk winds its way by the side of three meandering brooks in an area of typical Staffordshire countryside.

The village pub, Milwich.

Milwich is an unpretentious village with well tended gardens and is set in delightful countryside. All Saints' church is particularly attractive being set back from the road and is reputed to house the oldest bell in the country. The Green Man is the only pub in the village. It was built around the 15th century but did not become a public house until 1775 – a list of the names of licensees is on display inside.

The walk starts from the Green Man where opening hours tend to reflect the rural nature of the village and area. Bass, Worthington Best Bitter and a selection of guest ales are always available and Scrumpy Jack cider is also on tap. On Saturday the bar is open from 12 noon to 11 pm and on Sunday from 12 noon to 4 pm and 7 pm to 10.30 pm. From Wednesday to Friday of each week drinks are available from 12 noon to 4 pm and 5 pm to 11 pm, but the pub is open only in the evenings on Monday and Tuesday (again from 5 pm to 11 pm).

Typical walkers' food is prominent on the menu which offers a good selection of hot and cold bar snacks between 12 noon and 2 pm on Wednesday, Thursday and Friday and at weekends. On Thursday there is a special two-course set meal available at reasonable cost with coffee included. This traditional village inn provides a friendly haven for local residents and ramblers alike, and walking parties can be catered for by prior arrangement.

The Green Man has a super large garden area with picnic tables where dogs (under control) and children are very welcome. Children are also permitted in the pub for eating.

Telephone: 01889 505310.

- **HOW TO GET THERE:** Milwich is situated to the north-east of Stafford on the B5027 (Stone to Uttoxeter) road. The Green Man is in Sandon Lane in the centre of the village at the B5027 road junction with the Sandon road.
- **PARKING:** The Green Man has a large car park which is available to walking customers with the prior agreement of the licensee. Alternatively, park with care by the roadside in Milwich.
- **LENGTH OF THE WALK**: 3½ miles. Map: OS Pathfinder 830 – Stone (Staffs) (GR 972323).

THE WALK

1. From the Green Man, go left along the pavement of the B5027 road. In 50 yards, cross over the road and go right to walk through a close of residential houses to a T-junction at its end. Cross over the road and proceed ahead following a finger post to walk the farm drive to the right of Manor Farm. Exit the farm complex through a gate into pastureland and bear left to walk along the bank of Wheatlow Brook as it meanders north. Initially you will walk on the right bank of the brook and then after about 350 yards go over a stile/footbridge to continue on the left bank. Continue over two fields and then go over a hedge-stile to descend a farm track over the brook.

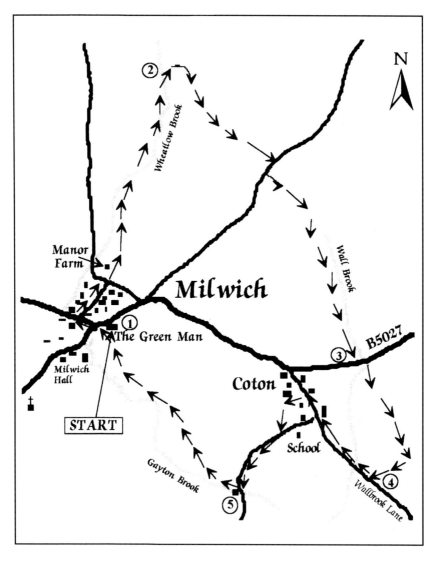

2. After crossing the brook, go right through a gate and now proceed south-east over pleasant Staffordshire countryside. You will gently ascend through a gate to go over a stile onto a lane. Here, go right then in 50 yards go left to continue in a generally south-east direction, crossing over a track called Darley Lane then continuing over pastureland to walk by Wall Brook. You will eventually go over a stile onto the B5027 road.

3. Cross over the road and continue through a gate. After walking over pleasant fields for about 500 yards you will reach a further stile. Do not go over this stile but turn around and now aim for a pair of midfield gates in line with Coton Green Farm. Proceed through the gates, now going north-west to the top corner of the next field to arrive on Wallbrook Lane.

4. Go right and walk the lane into the tiny hamlet of Coton. At Firs House go left through a farm gate, bearing left to go through a second gate into a field. Aim for a stile to the right of a metal farm gate – you will see a small school building to the left. Go over the stile into Mill Lane and then go right to walk past Beacon View Cottage. As the lane bends to the left, go right at a finger post to walk to the right of a farm-type building.

5. Initially you will walk very close to Gayton Brook and then will veer right to walk along a path to the right of a hedgerow. The path proceeds north-west over several fields and stiles as it meanders by Gayton Brook to emerge over a stile into the picnic garden of the Green Man.

Places of Interest Nearby
Sandon Hall on the A51 ($2\frac{1}{2}$ miles from Milwich) is the ancestral home of the Earl of Harrowby. It houses a unique collection of memorablia. Telephone: 01889 508004.

THE RIVER DOVE AT TUTBURY

This delightful short walk combines a stroll along the banks of the beautiful River Dove with a meander through the old streets of historic Tutbury.

The Leopard, Tutbury.

Tutbury, originally known as Totta's Burgh, was a fortified place in the Saxon kingdom of Mercia and was recorded in the Domesday Book as being one of only three burghs in the county – and the only one to have a market. The town has attracted a number of skilled craftsmen and women. Spare time to visit some of them – the local artists, a clockmaker, jewellery makers, wrought iron workers and glass engravers provide a fascinating display of skills for one to enjoy. Tutbury Glass is probably the most famous and at their premises one can see glass being blown into shape. Set upon the hill overlooking Tutbury are the ruins of Tutbury Castle – its most famous royal visitor was Mary Queen of Scots who was imprisoned in the castle on three occasions while she was held at the mercy of Elizabeth I.

The walk starts from the Leopard public house, an early 20th-century inn which is sited close to Tutbury Castle and is a convenient location for this waterside walk and close to the places of interest in the old town. Walkers will receive a warm welcome at the Leopard which is open from 11 am to 11 pm at weekends when Top Hat real ale and a variety of guest ales can be enjoyed in a village pub atmosphere. During the week drinks are available from 11 am to 3 pm and from 6 pm to 11 pm. The cider drinker will be pleased that Strongbow is on tap or perhaps a glass of wine may be your choice. A full bar menu is on offer during opening hours and walking parties can be served their own favourite foods by making prior arrangements.

Dogs (on leads) and children are allowed inside and there are picnic tables at the front of the pub from which one can watch the world go gently by.

Telephone: 01283 813170.

- **HOW TO GET THERE:** Tutbury is situated about 4 miles to the north-west of Burton upon Trent. The A50 road passes through the town and Monk Street is easily found by following the road signs to 'Free Car Park'. The Leopard public house is opposite the car park.
- **PARKING:** Adequate parking is always available in the town's large free car park (with toilets) in Monk Street.
- **LENGTH OF THE WALK:** 2 miles. Map: OS Pathfinder 852 – Burton upon Trent (GR 211289).

THE WALK

1. From the Leopard, ascend the pavement of Castle Street. Where Castle Street becomes Park Lane, go right onto a footpath between buildings to reach a couple of stiles onto open countryside. You will descend the pastureland of Castle Hill and can proceed on a clear path, going over a footbridge and a couple of stiles to reach the River Dove. At the river, go sharp right to cross a stile and reach an attractive weir. It is this weir which lets water into the stream known as Mill Fleam which in turn feeds the old cornmill situated on the other side of Tutbury.

2. Cross the footbridge to the weir and now walk a well worn path along the banks of the beautiful River Dove as it meanders east. There is a waymarked footpath to your right which runs

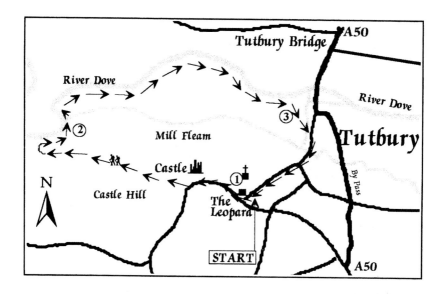

by the water-plant covered Fleam but the Dove's river bank is a delightful alternative which has been walked for many years. As you near the field hedge the path veers right to a stile by Tutbury Cricket Pitch to enter a landscaped picnic area with car park. This was the site of Tutbury Mill, which once produced cotton and later converted locally mined gypsum into plaster – it closed in 1968 and has been converted into a leisure and recreation area for Tutbury people.

3. Walk along the entrance lane to reach the A50 road and Bridge Street. Go right to pass the road island and meander up Bridge Street into Tutbury. Bear left to continue up High Street where you will pass by several antique shops and Ye Olde Dog & Partridge Inn – an olde worlde street indeed. At its end go right along Duke Street to reach the car park at the Monk Street corner.

Places of Interest Nearby

Tutbury Crystal Glass, Burton St, Tutbury – visitors can see fine crystal being made and cut in the factory. Telephone: 01283 813281. *Sudbury Hall* (about 5 miles north-west of Tutbury) – a fine 17th-century house with rich interior decoration and ceilings. Telephone: 01283 585305.

HIGH OFFLEY AND THE SHROPSHIRE UNION CANAL

A walk along the towpath of the Shropshire Union Canal in this delightful part of Staffordshire is always a pleasure. This easy circuit starts from the historic Anchor Inn by the side of the canal and leads below the pleasant village of High Offley before reaching the waterside again to visit the amazing bridge No 39 which contains a telegraph pole within its structure. The walk concludes with a gentle canalside walk back to the inn.

The 'Telegraph' Bridge.

High Offley is a remote and peaceful village set in attractive Staffordshire farming countryside. The word Offley comes from the medieval word Offleie – an extensive tract of land. This tract of land is bisected by the Shropshire Union Canal which is overlooked by a 700 year old village church imperiously planted on a hilltop in the village.

The Anchor Inn, sited on the banks of the canal, was built in

1827 to provide refreshments for canal workers and bargees when the canal was first built by Thomas Telford. This veritable treasure of an inn has retained its simple alehouse character and still holds its original furnishings which include settles and tables. It has been in the family of the current landford for some 100 years.

Walkers are always welcome at the Anchor where Wadworth 6X is the real ale on hand pump. Weston's cider is also on pump and comes sweet, medium or dry. The walker's food needs are met by a mixture of sandwiches and toasties with a variety of fillings – ham, cheese and salmon are the most popular. Drinks and food are available whenever the inn is open. In summer months the opening times are 11 am to 3 pm and 6 pm to 11 pm from Monday to Saturday, 12 noon to 3 pm and 7 pm to 10.30 pm on Sunday. In winter the inn is only open for specific limited periods – on Friday evening from 7 pm to 11 pm, Saturday from 11 am to 3 pm and 7 pm to 11 pm and Sunday from 12 noon to 3 pm and 7 pm to 10.30 pm.

The picnic garden by the side of the canal is ideal for the family and there is a gift shop (open on request at any time of the day) which offers T-shirts and towels depicting the Shropshire Union Canal. A camping and caravanning area is adjacent to the inn. Dogs on leads are permitted inside.

Telephone: 01785 284569.

- **HOW TO GET THERE:** High Offley is situated to the south-west of Stoke-on-Trent and is reached on the A519 to the south of Eccleshall. The Anchor Inn is on the canal bank in Peggs Lane and to reach it drive westwards past the church in High Offley and take the next left turn – the inn is on the left just after you cross the canal bridge.
- **PARKING:** The Anchor has a large car park which may be used by walkers who patronise the inn. Alternatively, park with care near the church.
- **LENGTH OF THE WALK:** 4 miles. Map: OS Pathfinder 849 – Hodnet and Norbury (GR 775256).

THE WALK

1. From the car park at the Anchor Inn, descend to the towpath of the Shropshire Union Canal and go left under Anchor Bridge (No 42). Walk the pleasant towpath until you reach

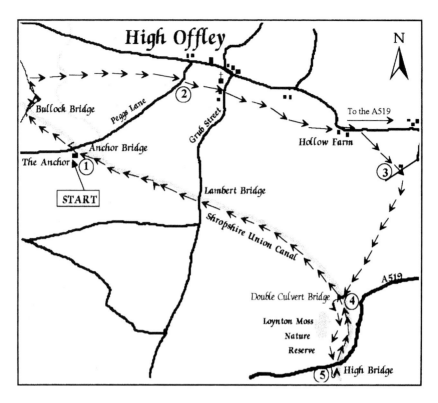

Bullock Bridge (No 43) where you leave the canal and go over the bridge on a wide track. In about 70 yards the track veers left to enter a cultivated field. In 150 yards go right across the field aiming (east) for a footbridge into the next field. Now continue on your walk line aiming for a gate at the field top right hand corner and proceed to the right of the hedge of the next field to arrive at a stile onto Peggs Lane.

2. Go over the stile at the other side of Peggs Lane, then cross over the next field with the village church proud on the hill to the left and a pleasing view of the countryside to the right. Proceed over stiles to go over Grub Street and continue on the clear path which now bears generally south-east, following to the right of hedges. You will go over a few stiles and through a gap in a hedge before arriving over a stile and gate onto the road near Hollow Farm. Walk past Hollow Farm and, in about 90 yards, go right over a hedge-stile into pastureland. Continue

to the right of the hedge until you reach a rather dilapidated car repair area.

3. Bear left, then go right onto a waymarked path. As you reach open land, aim south-west for a stile positioned to the left of a sycamore tree and then walk the very clear path over fields towards a building. At the fence, go left through a gate then sharp right to walk through a copse to reach the Shropshire Union Canal at Double Culvert Bridge.

4. Cross over the canal bridge and go left to enter Loynton Moss Nature Reserve – Loynton Moss is mentioned in the Domesday Book, having been formed in the Ice Age about 10,000 years ago. As you walk through the pleasant woodland look out for common reed, greater reedmace and the lesser celandine. You may also be lucky enough to spot a sedge warbler or a speckled wood butterfly. At the end of the woodland descend to the A519 road and go through the gate opposite to reach the towpath of the Shropshire Union Canal. As soon as you reach the towpath, go left and admire the unique telegraph pole bridge (No 39). It is the sole survivor of the many lines which once existed on the canal banks.

5. Proceed under the bridge and walk along the towpath by the side of the canal, passing beneath two more bridges as you return to the Anchor Inn by bridge No 41.

Places of Interest Nearby
Eccleshall (5½ miles) is an attractive, colourful historic town – a couple of old coaching inns, Hilcote Valley Railway and Rob Smith's Birds of Prey and Wildlife Sanctuary. *Dorothy Clive Garden*, Willoughbridge, Market Drayton (about 12 miles to the north-west of High Offley) – fine gardens with delightful views. Telephone: 01630 647237.

THE TRENT WASHLANDS AND BURTON UPON TRENT

The Trent Washlands are attractive low-lying lands adjacent to the River Trent which have been recognised for their value to leisure and wildlife – they comprise open meadows, wetlands, woods and waterways. This short and easy walk starts near Ferry Bridge and offers the delights of natural waterside country together with an opportunity to visit the historic parts of Burton upon Trent.

Ferry Bridge.

Burton upon Trent has, since the Middle Ages, been known as the home of British brewing and still produces its beer in individual barrels. Michael Bass, who became Lord Burton in the 19th century, gave the town many of its finest buildings including the town hall and the churches of St Paul and St Modwen. The River Trent passes through the town and is crossed by three bridges.

One of the great pleasures Burton can offer is to sit on a picnic bench by the River Trent with a glass in hand while admiring a superb 19th-century bridge and watching the world go by. The Boathouse Inn at Stapenhill invites walkers to enjoy a day by the Trent Washlands – and is also a good place to while away an hour, or three. Seven real ales are available including Boathouse Bitter, Marston's Pedigree, Bass and Abbot. Carling lager and Scrumpy Jack are on tap too, while wine can be taken by the glass or bottle. The bar is open for long hours at weekends: on Saturday from 11.30 am to 11 pm and on Sunday from 12 noon to 10.30 pm. During the week drinks are available from 11.30 am to 3 pm and from 5.30 pm to 11 pm.

Superb food is served in the first floor restaurant, in the bar area or at the picnic tables by the river. At lunchtime the Meat & Eat Menu is particularly popular and steak and kidney pudding is served every Wednesday – but do look on the specials board as well. An à la carte menu is available for those who seek a little extra luxury, and a window table in the restaurant will make for a very special occasion. The Boathouse is a popular eating place and booking is required for Sunday. Food is served on Saturday from 12 noon to 9.30 pm, on Sunday from 12 noon to 9 pm and on weekdays from 12 noon to 3 pm and 6.30 pm to 9.30 pm. Dogs (on leads) and children are welcome inside the inn.

Telephone: 01283 538831.

- **HOW TO GET THERE:** Burton upon Trent is situated on the east side of Staffordshire. The Trent Washlands are to the south of the town and are best approached on the A444 road. At the road island near to St Peter's church, drive into Main Street. In about 100 yards, go right into Ferry Street then go right again into a narrow lane called The Dingle which leads to the Boathouse Inn.
- **PARKING:** The Boathouse offers free car parking to its walking customers. There is also a public car park in Stapenhill Road, just past St Peter's church.
- **LENGTH OF THE WALK:** 3 miles. Map: OS Pathfinder 852 – Burton upon Trent (GR 253219).

THE WALK

1. Start the walk from the Boathouse Inn by walking over the superb Ferry Bridge (opened in 1889 when there was a toll of ½d per person) and proceed over Stapenhill Viaduct (a raised walkway which was a gift from the Baron of Burton in 1889).

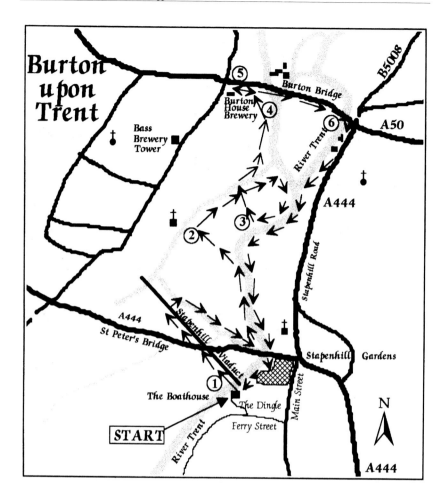

This delightful walk offers pleasant views over the surrounding Trent Washlands. Just before the end of the viaduct, go right and descend onto a tarmac path and cross a footbridge over The Silverway. Go right and walk by the side of The Silverway stream to reach the River Trent. Continue on the tarmac path now by the side of the Trent and then go left to walk to the right of rugby football pitches to reach The Cherry Orchard play and picnic area.

2. Proceed past The Cherry Orchard to reach the riverside near to St Modwen's church (on the other side of the Trent). Bear

Swans and ducks looking to be fed on the Trent.

right and walk past Andresey Bridge and a further bridge now on a grass path which circles right past a sculpture.

3. Where the grass path meets a tarmac path, go sharp right and cross Andresey Island on the tarmac path, aiming for the huge Bass Brewery Tower. Go over the bridge. Now bear right and walk along the river bank to the weir by Burton Bridge (opened in 1964) – this makes for a photo opportunity.

4. Ascend the path up to the A50 road and go left along the pavement to enter Bridge Street and to see the Burton Bridge Inn. This has parts dating from the 17th century and is the second oldest remaining public house in Burton. The Burton Bridge Brewery was established in 1982 to cater for an increasing demand for real ale and has won many awards for excellence. The inn is a small, friendly brewery taproom that sells five or six Burton Bridge beers – a chance to taste a locally brewed real ale.

5. Leave Burton Bridge Inn and walk over Burton Bridge on its wide footpath with a good overhead view of the weir.

6. At the bridge end, go right and walk along the pavement of

the A444 road. You will pass the blue boathouse of Burton upon Trent Sea Cadet Corps and Burton Leander Rowing Club before bearing right to walk on a path by the side of the River Trent once more. The tarmac path meanders along the bank of the river passing Stapenhill Hollows, a car park and then St Peter's church. Soon you will walk beneath St Peter's Bridge (built 1985) to enter the beautiful Stapenhill Pleasure Gardens – a true picture with colourful flowerbeds. Continue on the path and you will all too soon arrive back at the Boathouse Inn to enjoy refreshment at one of the riverside picnic tables.

Places of Interest Nearby
The Bass Museum in Horninglow Street is a must visit place. Telephone: 01283 511000.

The Boathouse Inn at Stapenhill.

STAFFORD'S HERITAGE AND THE RIVER SOW

❦

A short walk by the side of the River Sow leading into the centre of Stafford to wander among its most impressive heritage. A delightful day visit to the lovely county town.

The pub in Victoria Square, Stafford.

Stafford is a fascinating town to meander around. Its history goes back some 1,200 years and it is mentioned in the Domesday Book as a borough. It had a market as long ago as 1230 and has been represented in Parliament since 1295. The whole world knows of Stafford through the renowned angler Izaak Walton, who was born there in 1593. He was baptised in St Mary's church and in the north aisle there is a bust inscribed 'Izaak Walton, Piscator'. Charles I and Prince Rupert stayed in the magnificent Ancient High House in 1642 while recruiting. This walk will take you past these buildings and also the Shire Hall, the Swan Hotel and St Chad's church.

The route starts from the Riverside Recreation Centre, and the Bird in Hand pub is situated in Victoria Square, about halfway round the circuit, a good place for refreshment before you start exploring Stafford's town centre. Built in the early 19th century, this attractive coaching house offers a warm welcome to visitors to the county town. The super range of real ales includes Courage Directors and Best, John Smith's Yorkshire Bitter, Worthington Best and a guest beer. These plus Taunton sweet and dry ciders and French house wines are available between 11 am and 11 pm from Monday to Saturday and between noon and 10.30 pm on Sundays.

A full bar menu is served all the time the pub is open from Monday to Saturday (no food on Sundays) and there is a specials board. The home-made cheese and potato pie is very popular with regulars and visitors alike.

Children are allowed inside and in the large beer garden at the back. The only dogs allowed in are guide dogs. Families will particularly enjoy their visit to the Bird in Hand where there is a large separate games room with pool tables and electronic games for those who have energy to spare.

Telephone: 01785 252198.

- **HOW TO GET THERE:** Stafford lies at the junction of the A34, A513 and A518 roads. The Riverside Recreation Centre will be found on the north bank of the River Sow.
- **PARKING:** Park in one of the pay & display car parks near to the Riverside Recreation Centre.
- **LENGTH OF THE WALK:** 1½ miles. Map: OS Explorer 6 – Cannock Chase and Chasewater (GR 925230).

THE WALK

1. From the Riverside Recreation Centre, descend towards the bank of the River Sow. Then go right and walk along the footpath above the flowerbox-lined river to reach Greengate Street. Cross over Greengate Street with care and walk towards the town centre. At the crossroads, go left into Mill Bank and walk past Seamus O'Donnell's (on the corner) and the Coach & Horses then enter Victoria Park (opened in 1908) on the left to walk by the river – the park incorporates an old mill and weir. The town mill produced animal feeds until 1957 when it ceased to operate. The second of the gardens by the riverside is a picture with border flowers and several ornamental statues.

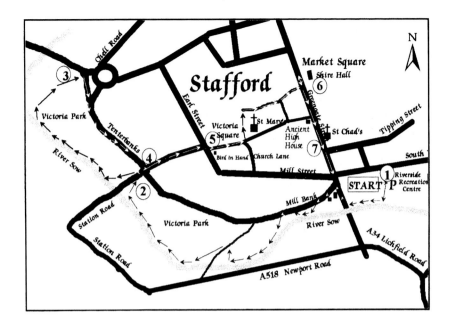

Keep by the water and you will probably see young people in canoes and many birds on the reedy river. At the end of the gardens you will emerge onto Station Road.

2. Cross over Station Road on the zebra crossing and enter a larger area of Victoria Park. The walk on the river bank offers a peaceful stretch of walking and to your right you will pass a large children's paddling area – it is a delight to watch youngsters splashing happily there in summer.

3. Exit the park by the road island and take time to look at Broad Eye Windmill – this was built in 1796 by John Wright whose initials are on the mill. The mill was constructed with recycled stone from the old Shire Hall and became steam driven by 1847 but ceased to be used after 1880. Now return to walk along the footpath of Tenterbanks and then cross the road at the light crossing. Go right and continue until you reach the small road island opposite Station Road.

4. Go left through the pedestrianised area to reach Earl Street. Cross over Earl Street and enter Victoria Square and there on

Victoria Park.

the street corner is the inviting picture of the Bird in Hand pub.

5. You will see that St Mary's church is the centrepiece of the square but before entering the church meander down the narrow and picturesque Church Lane which has a number of timbered buildings.

St Mary's collegiate church was begun in 1190 with later additions. A major restoration took place from 1841-44. There are several noteworthy features: the perpendicular octagonal crossing tower, a fine north transept with decorated doorway and windows, an unusual font and the tomb chest of Sir Edward Aston of Tixall.

At the rear of St Mary's descend the passageway to the right of The Grove Coffee Shop to reach Market Square in the main pedestrianised area of Stafford.

6. There in front of you is the Shire Hall, designed by John Harvey (a student of Samual Wyatt). The hall was built in 1798 to replace an Elizabethan building. Initially it was occupied as an assize court and also for meetings and dances. Today the hall is one of Staffordshire's most attractive historic buildings, containing a gallery and craft shop but still retaining the original panelled courtrooms.

Leaving the Shire Hall, go left and walk down the pedestrianised shopping street into Greengate Street to visit the Ancient High House.

The Ancient High House was built in 1595 by the Dorrington family and is the largest timber-framed town house in England. This magnificent building will have you reaching for your camera and its history will fascinate. In the 18th century Richard Sneyd lived in the house, but it later became a high class grocer's shop. Sadly, by 1970 the house was in a poor state of repair and it was then that Stafford Borough Council rescued this part of the county's heritage. Today the Ancient High House contains a museum, gift shop and the tourist information centre.

Near to the Ancient High House is the Swan Hotel – an old coaching inn. In the 18th century horse-drawn coaches and carriages would call in on their way to Manchester, Bristol, Chester, London. Liverpool or Birmingham. One can imagine the scene and the carriage entrance is still visible. Charles Dickens stayed at the Swan Hotel in 1852.

As you proceed down Greengate Street note St Chad's church on the left. Begun about 1150 this is the oldest church in Stafford and is a good example of a small Norman parish church. Although extensively restored in the 19th century, the building retains its Norman character.

7. Continue along Greengate Street, passing by Mill Street and then going left just before the bridge to return to the car park via the attractive flower-adorned footpath.

Places of Interest Nearby
Stafford Castle is the site of a Norman fortress. There is a visitor centre, a herb garden and a museum of arms and armour. Telephone: 01785 257698. *Izaak Walton Cottage* is a picturesque black and white 16th-century thatched cottage with historic displays. Izaak Walton is best remembered for writing *The Compleat Angler* in 1653. Telephone: 01785 760278.

GREAT HAYWOOD AND THE MEETING OF CANALS

Without doubt this is one of the finest waterside walks in Staffordshire and a treat for any walker. The circuit starts from a picturesque lane in the village of Great Haywood then follows the towpath of the Trent & Mersey Canal to a meeting with the Staffordshire & Worcestershire Canal. After more canalside walking the route ascends to pass the superb Shugborough Hall before returning to Great Haywood over the River Trent and the Trent & Mersey.

Tixall Lock.

Shugborough Hall was built in 1693 and later enlarged by Thomas Anson. The wings were added about 1748 and then, in 1794, the eight-columned portico was built to complete a superb façade. The inside of this National Trust property is richly decorated with fine rococo plasterwork and there are splendid collections of 18th-century ceramics, silverware, paintings and French furniture.

As one walks past the drive/entrance to Shugborough Farm Museum, the Arch of Hadrian will catch the eye. This copy of Hadrian's Arch in Athens was built for Thomas Anson in 1761 on the site of the original village of Shugborough. The arch, which contains the bust of Admiral Lord Anson and his wife, was intended to celebrate Anson's circumnavigation of the world in 1740–44.

Where better to start such a fine walk than the Clifford Arms in Great Haywood! This delightful pub, which has all of the facilities needed by a walker, is ideally situated near the entrance to the Trent & Mersey Canal. In summer the black and white frontage is an inviting vision, being adorned with hanging flower baskets. Sadly the original old coaching hotel building was destroyed by fire in the 1930s but was quickly rebuilt, in part using Italian POW labour. The superb parquet floor in the bar/lounge was built by the Italians and has been lovingly restored to form a feature for all to admire and enjoy. The licensee and his wife are rightly proud of their renovated property and offer a warm and cheerful welcome to those walking the nearby waterways. The bar is open for drinks from 12 noon to 11 pm during the week. On Saturdays it is open from 11.30 am to 11 pm while on Sundays 12 noon to 10.30 pm are the bar hours. Four real ales are featured and dry and sweet ciders are on draught.

Scrumptious bar food is available every day throughout the year – from 12 noon to 3 pm and from 6 pm to 9.30 pm – and Italian and Asian dishes are a speciality of the house. This is a popular pub and booking is advisable on Sundays during the summer.

There is a large, well-equipped garden with swings and facilities for children who are allowed in the pub when dining with their family. While dogs are welcome they are restricted to the front garden.

Telephone: 01889 881321.

- **HOW TO GET THERE:** Great Haywood is situated to the east of Stafford and is just west of the A51 between Lichfield and Weston. The Clifford Arms is in Main Road.
- **PARKING:** The Clifford Arms has a large car park for patrons. Because of its popular location, please telephone the licensee in advance to make specific arrangements if you wish to leave your

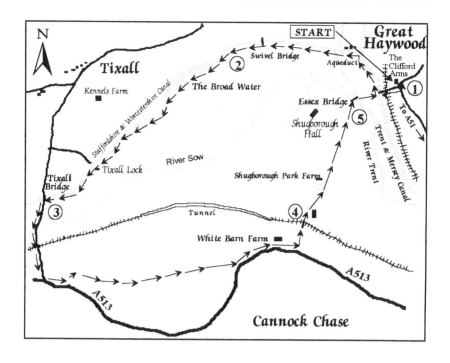

car there while walking. Alternatively, park by the roadside in Great Haywood, but do be considerate to the local people.

- **LENGTH OF THE WALK**: 4 miles. Map: OS Explorer 6 – Cannock Chase and Chasewater (GR 997226).

THE WALK

1. From the Clifford Arms, go right and then right again to walk along a short but picturesque lane beneath a railway bridge. Continue over bridge No 73 of the Trent & Mersey Canal and go left through a hand-gate onto the canal towpath then go left under bridge 73 to walk past Haywood Lock. There are normally a large number of narrowboats and small motor boats moored along this stretch of the towpath. Go left under an elegant sweeping arch bridge at Great Haywood Junction – a bridge made famous by the photography of canal historian Eric de Maré. Here the Staffordshire & Worcestershire Canal crosses the River Trent on an aqueduct to join the Trent & Mersey Canal. Narrowboats all congregate along this stretch of the canal where repair facilities are available. Continue along

Shugborough Hall.

the towpath of the Staffordshire & Worcestershire, passing the canal life of the narrowboat people as you walk beneath a swivel bridge (No 108) to reach Tixall Wide.

2. Tixall Wide is a 950 foot stretch of the canal which was deliberately widened to form a sort of lake to the former Tixall Hall. Today one can still see the massive 16th-century gatehouse (one of the largest in the UK) – it is three storeys in height, richly decorated with Roman, Ionic and Corinthian columns, and has four impressive tall turrets and, without knowing the history, one could have the impression that the gatehouse is an old folly. Yet more craft will no doubt be moored in Tixall Wide and fishing from narrowboats will be part of the scene as you walk past.

    Continue along the towpath beneath Oldhill Bridge (No 107) to reach Tixall Lock.

3. Exit the towpath at bridge No 106 and go left over Tixall Bridge on the roadside, over the River Sow and a railway bridge as you ascend a pavement to Milford Common.

    At the A513 road, go left and walk past the main entrance to Shugborough Hall, with its pair of fine Milford Lodges (1800), and continue along the side of its wall. At the wall end, go left and ascend a fairly steep path to the right of the wall. This is very pleasant countryside albeit via a short hill. At the top of the hill walk past a raised reservoir (enclosed in railings) and take the path ahead (do not take the path to the left) through attractive trees and ferns. Maintain your direction and descend through the Stafford Plantation to reach the A513 road once again where you go left and walk on the footpath. You will pass the entrance to Shugborough Working Farm Museum and after about 350 yards go left over a stile on a path which joins the driveway to the Farm Museum.

4. Bear right to go around the museum complex then continue ahead along a fenced tarmac track for a fine view of the magnificent building of Shugborough Hall on your left.

5. Shortly after passing the tradesmen's entrance to the Hall, go over the superb 16th-century packhorse bridge – Essex Bridge. It has 14 fine arches, is just 4 feet wide and offers a great photo opportunity as twin forks of the River Trent join beneath it. Because the bridge was not wide enough to carry a horse and carriage, the Anson family had a wider bridge built about 95 yards downstream to avoid having to walk some 270 yards to church each Sunday!

After crossing Essex Bridge walk over the canal bridge to arrive back in Great Haywood. Go left at Main Road to the Clifford Arms.

Places of Interest Nearby
Shugborough Hall is set in 900 acres of gardens and parkland – the Hall is the seat of Lord Lichfield. Telephone: 01889 881388. *Cannock Chase* comprises some 3,000 acres of attractive heath and woodlands where there is exceptionally fine walking.

PICTURESQUE ALREWAS AND ITS WATERWAYS

This easy circuit starts in the lovely village of Alrewas and features a route past two fine churches, a narrow lock and a pretty weir by the Trent & Mersey Canal. The return leg provides an invigorating walk along the banks of the River Trent.

The Crown Inn, Alrewas.

Alrewas is one of the prettiest black and white villages in Staffordshire and it is a delight to meander past the Tudor thatched cottages which line its wide main street. It is a very old village and prior to the arrival of the Romans a settlement already existed here. For many centuries it was famous for its eel fishery and for basket weaving but there is little evidence of this today. All Saints' church was built in the 13th/14th century to replace an earlier 9th-century building and it contains a 14th-century font adorned with four grotesque heads.

The Crown, situated in Post Office Road, is a dream picture pub adorned with beautiful flowers and it is little wonder that it has been Midlands winner of the 'Pub in Bloom' competition. Built in the 15th century this is a hostelry full of character and history – until 1860 one snug room was used as a post distribution room. Today a local artist has added fascinating paintings to the walls in the dining room and the back garden and has painted a narrowboat on the back wall of the large car park. Marston's Pedigree, Bass and guest ales (which are changed every two weeks) are available from 11 am to 3 pm and 5 pm to 11 pm from Monday to Saturday. On Sundays the bar is open from 12 noon until 3 pm and 7 pm to 10.30 pm. Strongbow cider is on tap and wine can be bought by the glass or by the bottle.

A full menu of bar snacks is offered (there is also a specials board) from 12 noon until 2 pm and 6 pm to 9.30 pm from Monday to Saturday. Home-made steak pies, lasagne and the Crown mixed grills are favourites with the locals. On Sundays food is served from 12 noon until 2.30 pm and from 7 pm to 9 pm.

Children are welcome in the pub as well as in the large garden at the rear. Dogs may be brought inside too if they are under control. It is possible for walkers to eat their own sandwiches in the garden if they purchase drinks in the pub.

Telephone: 01283 790328.

- **HOW TO GET THERE:** Alrewas is situated about 8 miles north-east of Lichfield, just off the A38 Lichfield to Burton upon Trent road. The Crown is in Post Office Road.
- **PARKING:** Walkers may leave their cars in the large car park at the Crown. Alternatively, space is available by the roadside near the post office.
- **LENGTH OF THE WALK**: 3 miles. Map: OS Pathfinder 872 – Rugeley and Lichfield (North) (GR 171152).

THE WALK

1. From the Crown car park, go left down Post Office Road to reach the main street in Alrewas. Go right and cross the bridge over the Trent & Mersey Canal, then go right to enter and

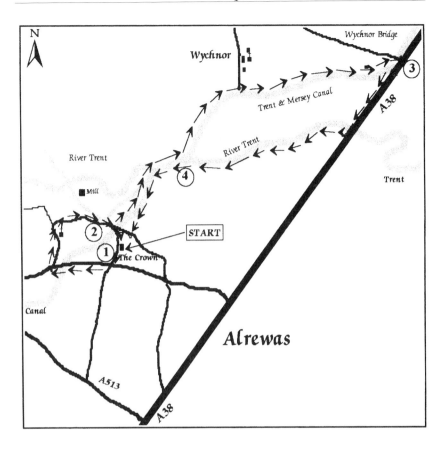

walk along Mill End Lane just above the canal. Proceed through the lychgate to enter All Saints' churchyard and to visit the historic church. Leave the churchyard via a gate behind the church to arrive in Church Road. Now go right and walk to bridge No 48 over the canal and descend left to join the towpath.

2. Walk along the towpath for just over a mile to reach the A38 road. Initially you will walk past moored boats and then go over a series of footbridges. After you have passed lock No 12 you will see that the River Trent flows in from the left and for some 200 yards the river and the canal are one. The river continues east over a weir while you stay on the towpath to reach Cow Bridge below the village of Wychnor where there

are more boat moorings. On August Bank Holiday each year there is a boat rally at Wychnor when very many colourful boats arrive to fill the canal. Go over the Wychnor Bridge (No 43) to arrive on the footpath of the A38.

3. Go right and walk along the footpath for about ½ mile. Immediately after going over the road bridge over the River Trent go right and descend the bank to walk on a footpath along the river bank. The path hugs the river as you go over a series of stiles and fences and Wychnor's St Leonard's church stands proud away to the right. This is a pleasant riverside walk and you are likely to see a variety of birds – among them swans, seagulls, moorhens and coots.

4. After passing the weir you will reach lock No 12 on the Trent & Mersey Canal, when the path veers away from the canal to go over a fence (by a farm gate) onto a wide track. The track becomes a lane and then you will arrive in Park Road in Alrewas. Go right and then turn left into Post Office Road to reach the Crown.

Places of Interest Nearby
Abbots Bromley and *Blithfield Reservoir* (about 12 miles to the north-west). Abbots Bromley is famous for the Horn Dance which takes place in September each year. The village centre has an attractive butter cross and there are several black and white pubs/cottages. The nearby reservoir is an angler's paradise and very pleasant to drive around.

WHITTINGTON AND THE COVENTRY CANAL

Near to the busy and yet very attractive cathedral city of Lichfield, Whittington is a small, unpretentious village. This easy walk meanders along the towpath of the delightful Coventry Canal in peaceful countryside and allows you to watch the world go by on colourful canal narrowboats.

The Coventry Canal.

The Coventry Canal was originally built to connect Coventry with the Trent & Mersey Canal and to transport cheap coal from Bedworth coalfield. The latter aim was achieved in 1769 but by the time the canal had reached Atherstone in 1771, all authorised building capital had been used up and James Brindley was sacked from the project. It was not until 1790 when the Coventry Canal finally reached Fradley via a link with the Birmingham and Fazeley Canal that the main canal artery link was completed.

The Swan inn is set on the very bank of the Coventry

Canal and its canalside garden is a superb place to start and finish a gentle walk in the Staffordshire countryside. In summer the front of the inn is adorned with flowers and walkers can be sure of a good welcome from the licensee in the comfortable bar area where drinks are available from 11.30 am to 3.30 pm and 5.30 pm to 11 pm during the week. On Saturday opening hours are from 11.30 am to 11 pm while on Sunday you will get drinks from 12 noon to 4 pm and from 7 pm to 10.30 pm. Ansells Bitter, Marston's Pedigree and one further real ale are always available and four-pint pitchers of beer can be taken into the garden – a fine way to spend a summer afternoon after a morning's walk. Strongbow cider will please the cider drinker while Stowell's of Chelsea wine is on draught. Bar food is available during drinking hours and the Swan has a full range of snacks which can be enjoyed in the bar or in the garden.

Children are very welcome and a large climbing frame is set up outside for their enjoyment – they are not allowed in the bar after 8 pm. Dogs (on leads please) can also accompany their owners inside the pub.

Telephone: 01543 432264.

- **HOW TO GET THERE:** Whittington is situated to the south-east of Lichfield and is just east of the A51 (Lichfield to Tamworth) road. The Swan is in Burton Road, near to the canal bridge.
- **PARKING:** The Swan has its own car park for the use of customers. Alternatively, you can park by the roadside in Whittington, but do be considerate to the local people.
- **LENGTH OF THE WALK:** 3 miles. Map: OS Pathfinder 892 – Lichfield and Brownhills (GR 162089).

THE WALK

1. From the Swan inn, go right to cross over the Coventry Canal Bridge (No 80). Go right and descend onto the towpath and walk along it for just over ½ mile to arrive at the Whittington Bridge. The towpath is a delight with a number of craft moored at the back of domestic properties and there are many interesting/attractive gardens to admire. Just before you reach the bridge you will walk a small stretch of the Birmingham & Fazeley Canal and there is a plaque to commemorate the joining of the two canals in July 1790.

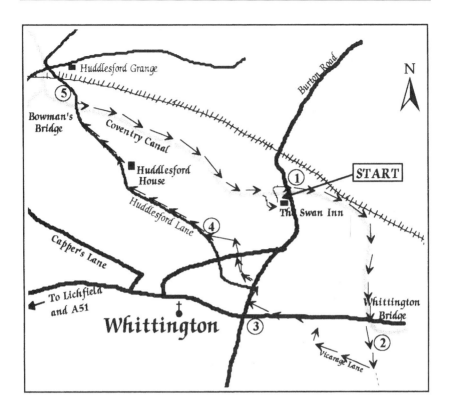

2. Go through the small gate and ascend onto the road. To the right, but almost opposite the bridge, is a wide farm track. Cross over the road and walk along this track by the side of a very productive strawberry field. At the track end, bear right onto Vicarage Lane which leads past a white cottage and playing fields. At the end of the playing field area, go right through a hand-gate and walk along the public path to reach Cloister Walk. Go left at the road and walk past Cloister Lodge and Whittington Old Hall to a road junction (Whittington Social Club is set on the right corner).

3. Go right past the Dog Inn and walk down the Main Street into Whittington. After about 150 yards, bear left and walk along Blacksmith's Lane, passing by some attractive town houses to reach a road.

   Cross over the road and walk along a hedged footpath to

The Swan, Whittington.

reach a cultivated field. Diagonally cross the field, aiming for its far left corner, to go over a stile onto Huddlesford Lane.

4. Walk to the right along the quiet lane, passing by the large complex of Huddlesford House and to your left you may catch a glimpse of the magnificent three-spired cathedral in Lichfield.

5. Cross over Bowman's Bridge and go right over a stile to rejoin the towpath of the Coventry Canal. Now walk on the towpath as it meanders through pleasant Staffordshire countryside, passing beneath bridge No 81. Leave the towpath at bridge No 80 and walk back to the Swan.

Places of Interest Nearby
Lichfield Cathedral City (3 miles) is one of the finest cities in the UK. It is famous for its wonderful three-spired cathedral and for being the birthplace of Dr Samuel Johnson, author of the very first comprehensive English dictionary. The city's grid pattern of streets with many timber-framed shops and houses has survived intact and there are gardens to explore. *Tamworth Castle* ($4\frac{1}{2}$ miles to the south-east of Whittington) is a Norman motte and bailey castle with one of the few remaining shell keeps in Britain. Telephone: 01827 63563.

THE SHROPSHIRE UNION CANAL AND BREWOOD

A fascinating medieval village is the finale to this delightful walk along the towpath of Thomas Telford's Shropshire Union Canal. Explore the flora of the area and spot the wide variety of birdlife by the canal then stroll around well-kept Brewood (pronounced 'Brood') and enjoy its fine range of historic buildings.

The Shropshire Union Canal, near Brewood.

Brewood, although just a few miles north of Wolverhampton, is a tranquil place, steeped in history. If you can tear yourself away from the ever absorbing canal, you will discover a village full of treasures. First established in Saxon times, Brewood is mentioned in the Domesday Book and, being situated in Brewood Forest, the village was visited by several early kings for royal hunting. A centre of Catholicism since the 16th century, the village was closely associated with the escape of Charles II after the battle of

Worcester in 1651. Brewood has retained much of its Georgian character and was designated an Outstanding Conservation Area in 1969. The oldest building (1350) is Old Smithy Cottages, but many that later catch the eye are 18th-century, for example, St Dominic's School (1798), the former workhouse, and Speedwell Castle (1740), an ornate Gothic house reputedly built by a local apothecary using his winnings on a horse called *Speedwell*. The old pump and horse trough in the attractive Market Place mark the site of the parish pump, and the church, with its altar tombs of the Catholic Giffard family of nearby Chillington Hall, is well worth a visit.

The walk starts from the Admiral Rodney where you will receive a friendly reception and will probably become a regular customer. Adorned with colourful hanging baskets in summer, this attractive Victorian public house was named after the famous naval hero of the 1780s who claimed never to have lost a battle. Located in the village it is a very convenient place from which to discover the treasures of Brewood.

Drinks are served from 11 am to 11 pm at weekends throughout the year while on weekdays the opening hours are from 12 noon to 3 pm and 5.30 pm to 11 pm. There is a wide selection of real ales – the Tipster's Choice range of beers, Tetley Bitter, Old Speckled Hen and Marston's Pedigree, with Dry Blackthorn cider on tap for the cider drinker.

The Admiral Rodney's menu offers all types of food from snacks to à la carte, including many home-cooked specials – the toasted baguettes are a treat for the walker in a hurry. Food is served from 12 noon until 9 pm at weekends, 12 noon to 3 pm and 6 pm to 9.30 pm on weekdays. It is pleasant to eat in the garden on warm days. There is also a private 'T' garden for afternoon teas available for group bookings.

Children in the company of adults are allowed in the pub, and dogs (under control).

Telephone: 01902 850583.

- **HOW TO GET THERE:** Brewood is situated to the north-west of Wolverhampton and is just west of Coven off the A449 (Wolverhampton to Stafford) road. The Admiral Rodney is in Dean Street.
- **PARKING:** Customers of the Admiral Rodney may leave their cars

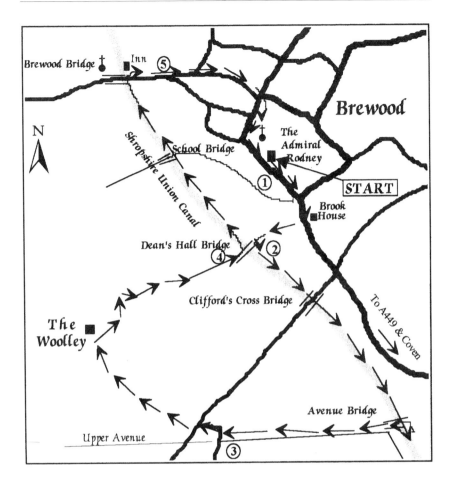

in the large car park while they walk. Alternatively, you can park by the roadside in Brewood, but do be considerate to the local people.

- **LENGTH OF THE WALK:** 3 miles. Map: OS Pathfinder 891 – Wolverhampton (North) (GR 884085).

THE WALK

1. From the car park at the Admiral Rodney, go left and descend Dean Street, crossing over the road to walk past Dean Street House (a 1792 building with tripartite windows) and Old Smithy Cottages. Go right opposite Brook House and walk a signed bridlepath lane which passes an algae-green pond then

proceed up to Dean's Hall Bridge for your first sight of the Shropshire Union Canal.

2. Go left (south-east) along the towpath of the canal, passing through pleasant countryside to reach Avenue Bridge. Initially walk beneath Avenue Bridge then turn round to admire the fine reflection of its unusual balustrade in the canal water. Ascend to the right of Avenue Bridge, then go left over the bridge to walk through the delightful tree-lined Lower Avenue. In about $\frac{1}{4}$ mile you will arrive at Park Lane.

    On another day you may choose to cross Park Lane and walk along Upper Avenue opposite to visit Chillington Hall.

3. Go right and walk up Park Lane to a road. Cross over the road and go through the farm gate opposite onto a wide track. Walk along this track, going north-west through a second gate and admiring the fine view of Brewood to your right. Soon you will reach a further farm gate which you go through and then bear right away from Hyde Farm. You are now on the Staffordshire Way and should pass to the right of Woolley Farm before bearing right to walk a hedged lane until you reach and cross Dean's Hall Bridge once again.

4. Leave the Staffordshire Way and descend to the Shropshire Union Canal. Now go right (north-west) along the towpath for a fine view of Brewood to your right. This pleasant stretch of canal walking will take you beneath School Bridge to arrive at Brewood Bridge where you should exit the towpath through a white gate to emerge in Brewood opposite the Bridge Inn.

5. Now go right to walk the pavement of High Green into the centre of Brewood, initially walking along Bargate Street and then bearing right into Market Place. Take your time and enjoy the many old buildings.

    As you enter Church Road, walk through the churchyard of Saint Mary and Saint Chad. Here you will find the grave of Colonel William Careless, the soldier who, after the battle of Worcester, hid King Charles II in the Royal Oak at nearby Boscobel House.

The Admiral Rodney, Brewood.

Leave the churchyard via a gate into Dean Street where you will pass yet more 18th-century buildings before you reach the Admiral Rodney.

Places of Interest Nearby

Chillington Hall (1½ miles south) – the home of the Giffard family since the 12th century. The Hall (built in the 18th century) and the gardens, landscaped by 'Capability' Brown in about 1730, are open to the public during the summer. The park is open all the year and is a favourite place for local walkers. Telephone: 01902 850397. *Cosford* (7½ miles to the south-west). The Aerospace Museum illustrates aviation through two world wars. Telephone: 01902 374872.

CHASEWATER AND ITS COUNTRY PARK

This easy walk starts in Chasetown, taking the walker over Chasetown Common for a gentle stroll around the lakeside and an attractive meander by the Anglesey Branch of the Wyrley & Easington Canal.

Chasewater Reservoir and pier.

There is great pleasure in walking around the beautiful lake of Chasewater – a 'must' day for the family. The 260 acre lake has become the largest water sports centre in the UK and there is always action to see and enjoy. The Cannock Sailing Club and the South Staffordshire Hydroplane and Speedboat Club entertain the visitor during summer months and there are pleasant walking paths to explore.

The Uxbridge Arms, not far from the Chasewater Reservoir, is a fine place to relax and enjoy a drink. Set on the edge of Chasetown, it was built in 1843 on land owned by the Earl of Uxbridge, the first Marquess of Anglesey. It has a good reputation with locals, who enjoy a variety of bar food and a wide selection of real ales. The pub offers a warm welcome to walkers throughout the year and in summer is a picture with hanging flower baskets adorning the front of the building. Drinks are available at weekends from 12 noon to 11 pm and during the week from 12 noon to 3 pm and from 5.30 pm to 11 pm. Bass, Highgate and a selection of guest ales from all over the country are always on tap as is Stowpress cider. You will enjoy the comfortable bar and lounge area.

Bar snacks include steaks, gammon, fish and home-made lasagne. Beef in beer and cold ham, eggs and chips are popular specials. Food is available from 12 noon to 2.15 pm and from 6 pm to 9 pm, apart from Sunday evenings.

Benches at the front and back of the pub provide a good location for children, who are always welcome but not in the bar area. Dogs are not allowed in the lounge but can be brought into the bar area if on leads.

Telephone: 01543 674853.

- **HOW TO GET THERE:** Chasetown is situated by Burntwood and is set to the north of the A5 road near Brownhills on the edge of the Black Country. The Uxbridge Arms is in Church Street – a Citroen dealer is sited on the opposite corner.
- **PARKING:** If you are a customer of the Uxbridge Arms you can use its car park while you walk. Alternatively, you can park by the roadside in Chasetown, but do be considerate to the local people.
- **LENGTH OF THE WALK:** 3 miles. Map: OS Pathfinder 892 – Lichfield and Brownhills (GR 043080).

THE WALK

1. From the Uxbridge Arms, go right up Church Street to pass by the cemetery and then Chasetown Primary School. Immediately past the school, go right onto a tarmac footpath into a grassy banked park-type area that leads into a residential road. Go left and walk along the path that proceeds at the back of houses to arrive on Chasetown Common at the back of factories. At the rear of the first factory ignore the pathways going to the left and proceed ahead to the left of the next complex of industrial buildings. Here, go ahead through a hedge gap and you will be immediately in attractive common countryside. Do not go left but continue ahead on a clear

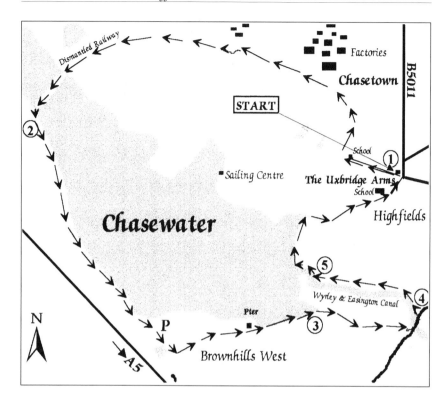

track that arcs left beneath overhead electric wires as the track joins a disused railway. This track will take you over a narrow stretch of land across Chasewater and from here you will enjoy a superb view of this fine lake.

2. At the lake bank go left again and now walk along the bank, arcing left by the side of Chasewater Light Railway to arrive by the large car parking area near the amusement park. Leave the water park by the car park exit and go left along a lane which leads to a bridge and the lake's dam wall – you will pass by the lake pier.

3. By the wall, go right onto a clear path/track which leads away from the lake, going generally east across moorland, covered in heather, to walk by the Wyrley & Easington Canal. This pleasant stretch of walking will take you to a bridge which you cross, going left.

4. At the end of the bridge, go left onto a path and now walk on the other bank of the canal. The pleasant, peaceful canal is now largely used by youngsters for fishing – one told me that the canal contains nice chub and that the biggest fish he had caught was a 21 pound pike! The canal meanders around the former Anglesey Wharf to return to Chasewater by the lake wall.

5. Go right and walk along the path by the side of the wall. From the path there is a fine view across the main lake and you will enjoy watching swans, ducks, moorhens, coots and maybe grebe on the water. At the wall end you will reach a lane. Cross and walk along the track to the right. This track bends right where there is a stile (on the left) onto a path through trees and fern to allow you to walk by the fence of school playing fields. You will emerge by Chasetown School and then enter Pool Road. Go left along Pool Road and at the corner with Church Street you will find the Uxbridge Arms.

Places of Interest Nearby
Wall Roman Site (south-east of Chasetown) was originally the Roman fort of Letocetum and was a military centre for some three decades from AD 50. It has the most complete Roman bath house in Britain. Telephone: 01543 480768.

THE BRATCH LOCKS WALK
AND TRYSULL

This easy walk starts in the attractive village of Trysull before passing through typical Staffordshire countryside to reach the Staffordshire & Worcestershire Canal and the famous Bratch Locks. You return to the village over fields and tracks.

Bratch Locks.

The Staffordshire & Worcestershire Canal stretches from the River Severn at Stourport on Severn to cross over the River Trent at Great Haywood junction in Staffordshire – a marvellous feat of James Brindley engineering which today is a treasured canal in the hearts of canal enthusiasts. In 1978, the whole canal was declared a Conservation Area preserving its many features of historic interest. One of the finest of these treasures is the Bratch Locks and there can be no better summer pleasure in West Staffordshire than to see ornate narrowboats negotiate the amazing 30'2" locks. Three locks set very close together by an attractive octagonal toll house combine to form a picture postcard sight.

The Plough Inn is situated in a quiet country lane in the nearby village of Trysull. It is a 300 year old inn, adorned with flowers in the summer and having every facility one could wish for. It has become a favourite with local people and attracts visitors from the surrounding area. The large garden has a barbecue and play area and it is a delightful spot in which to enjoy a lunch break in the country. The licensee is rightly proud of the inn and offers a cheerful, friendly welcome to walkers. Drinks are available from 11.30 am to 3 pm and 6 pm to 11 pm on weekdays, all day on Saturdays and from 12 noon to 3 pm and 7 pm to 10.30 pm on Sundays. Camerons Strong Arm and Marston's Pedigree real ales are supplied in the pleasant old bar area as well as Scrumpy Jack cider. The lounge has an interesting array of pictures including several of Lakeland.

A full menu of bar food is available from 12 noon to 2.30 pm and between 6 pm and 9 pm. Home-made steak and Guinness pie has my recommendation but there is a selection of daily specials to whet the appetite. Children are welcome and they will enjoy the excellent play area. Dogs are not allowed in the inn itself.

Telephone: 01902 892254.

- **HOW TO GET THERE:** Trysull is situated to the west of Wolverhampton just off the A449 (Kidderminster to Wolverhampton) road. The Plough Inn is in School Road just south of the church.
- **PARKING:** Walkers may leave their cars in the Plough's large car park if they are customers. Alternatively, either park with consideration by the roadside in Trysull near to All Saints' church (GR 852943) or, if you choose to walk from the Bratch Locks, there is a small car park by the picnic area at Bratch Bridge, Wombourne (GR 868937).
- **LENGTH OF THE WALK:** Just over 3½ miles. Map: OS Pathfinder 912 – Wolverhampton (South) (GR 851940).

THE WALK

1. From the Plough Inn car park, turn left and walk along School Road into Trysull. Pass by All Saints' church and go right into Bell Road. Go left in front of the very attractive 'The

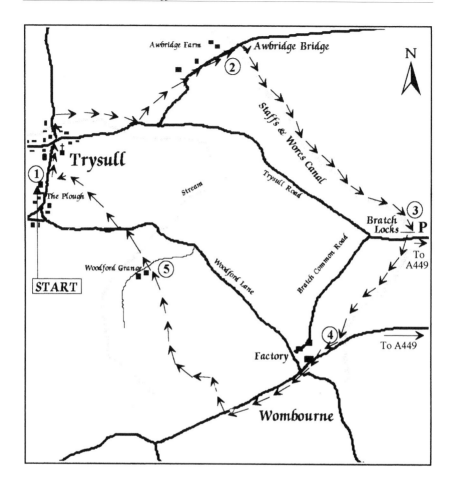

Thatchers' cottage and walk along Trysull Holloway. Just after crossing a bridge over a stream, go right on a footpath which meanders below a flower-laden cottage to go over a stile into pastureland. At the field end, go over a further stile then bear left to ascend a cultivated field, going beneath electric power lines to reach a lane corner. Proceed ahead and descend the lane, passing Orchard Cottage on the left to reach Awbridge Bridge.

2. Proceed over the old bridge and turn right to walk the left bank of the Staffordshire & Worcestershire Canal. This is a pleasant canalside stretch of walking where ducks, moorhens

Awbridge Bridge.

and coots may keep you company. You will pass a cricket pitch on the far bank just before reaching the moorings to the Bratch Locks – so many colourful narrowboats to admire.

3. Pause at the Bratch Locks to enjoy a very special experience then proceed over Bratch Bridge to walk along the towpath on the right bank of the canal. To your right below Bratch Common you will see an abundance of wildflowers in the wetlands which were once a small lake. Pass by Bumble Hole Lock and leave the canal by a narrow path at the next bridge to arrive in Poolhouse Road.

4. Ascend the pavement, passing the large Ferro factory on the right. At the brow of the hill walk along the footpath inside the road hedge by The Meadlands residential estate. In about ¼ mile, go through a hedge gap, cross over the Bridgnorth road and enter a waymarked disused road which is protected from vehicles by two very large boulders. Go through the side gate and walk the tarmac road which becomes a track as it bends left. Go over the field stile and aim for a second stile by a farm gate ahead, then continue the walking line which runs parallel with electric pylons to the right, now aiming to the right of Woodford Grange Farm.

5. Pass the farm buildings and their array of vehicles (under repair?) bearing left to walk along the driveway to Grange House. You will walk over a bridge across a stream – a delightful stretch of walking in the summer as you pass along a driveway of attractive wildflowers to reach a lane. At the lane, go left then, just past Woodford Cottage, go right through a hedge gap into a cultivated field. Cross the field, aiming north-west towards the tower of All Saints' church in Trysull. At the field corner, go through a hand-gate and walk along a hedged path to reach School Road – on your left will be the Plough Inn.

Places of Interest Nearby
Himley Hall, just to the south of Wombourne, is a Grade II listed building located in 180 acres of parkland with a fine lake. The Hall was once the home of the Earl of Dudley. Telephone: 01902 326665.

KINVER AND THE STAFFORDSHIRE & WORCESTERSHIRE CANAL

This easy scenic walk follows the towpath of the delightful Staffordshire & Worcestershire Canal between Kinver and Stewponey Locks and passes through a pretty bluebell wood by the side of the meandering River Stour. There are pleasant views to enjoy on the walk which ends with a stroll along Kinver's fascinating High Street.

Stewponey Lock.

A favourite beauty spot in the south-west corner of Staffordshire, the village of Kinver is renowned as being a centre for fine walking. Named Chenevare in the Domesday Book, there are a number of buildings of interest to enjoy. Spend time at St Peter's church and in the High Street, parts of which date back to medieval times – the White Hart Hotel and the Pharmacy are two of the buildings which helped the village win an Architectural Heritage Award in 1975. The Kinver Grammar School is a superb

16th-century half-timbered house although it is no longer a school.

Our walk starts from the Vine Inn, situated by Kinver Lock on the very banks of the Staffordshire & Worcestershire Canal. There can be few nicer ways to enjoy a summer evening or a weekend lunch than to sit outside with a drink and watch beautifully decorated canal barges negotiate the narrow lock. Built in 1771 for the workers on James Brindley's meandering contour canal, the white building is a picture in summer when it is adorned with colourful hanging flower baskets. The licensee offers a warm welcome to walkers in the cosy half-timbered bar area where drinks are served from 12 noon to 11 pm throughout the year. Hobsons, 6X, Enville and Worthington real ales together with two guest bitters are available and Strongbow, Blackthorn and Old Stowford Press ciders are all on draught.

A full menu of good bar food is offered from 12 noon to 2.30 pm and 6.30 pm to 10 pm on Monday to Friday. On Saturdays and Sundays food is available all day long. The large, well-presented portions attract local people as well as visitors and it is advisable to book for Sunday lunch in the summer.

Children are welcome and they will enjoy the play facilities and the large canalside garden where ducks and goats are kept. Dogs should be on leads.

Telephone: 01384 877291.

- **HOW TO GET THERE:** Kinver lies to the west of Stourbridge just off the A449 (Kidderminster to Wolverhampton) road. The Vine Inn is in Mill Lane by Kinver Lock Bridge.
- **PARKING:** Customers of the Vine Inn may leave their cars in the pub car park while walking although it does get rather crowded at peak times. Alternatively, there are several free car parks off the High Street in Kinver.
- **LENGTH OF THE WALK:** 4 miles. Map: OS Pathfinder 933 – Stourbridge and Kinver (GR 849835).

THE WALK

1. From the Vine Inn car park, turn right and cross Kinver Lock Bridge then go right again to walk on the towpath of the Staffordshire & Worcestershire Canal. Initially you will walk past the busy Kinver Lock (No 29) and then reach a mooring